MODERN JAPAN
A BRIEF HISTORY

ARTHUR E. TIEDEMANN
The City College of New York

AN ANVIL ORIGINAL
under the general editorship of
LOUIS L. SNYDER

D. VAN NOSTRAND COMPANY, INC.
PRINCETON, NEW JERSEY
TORONTO   LONDON
NEW YORK

TO MY PARENTS

———————————————

D. VAN NOSTRAND COMPANY, INC.

120 Alexander St., Princeton, New Jersey (*Principal office*)
24 West 40th Street, New York 18, New York
25 Hollinger Rd., Toronto 16, Canada
358, Kensington High Street, London, W.14, England

PREFACE

One of the most startling events of modern history was the meteoric rise of Japan. In 1853 she was an inconsequential country living two hundred and fifty years behind the times. A handful of foreign warships was enough to force humiliating treaties upon her. Fewer than a hundred years later she was the conqueror of East and Southeast Asia, and it required the mightiest air and and sea armadas the world had yet seen to bring her down to defeat. It is the aim of this book to give a brief but balanced account of the last hundred years of Japanese history. So that the reader may understand conditions in Japan on the eve of its opening, a short survey of the Tokugawa period (1600-1867) is also included.

In two ways Japan has an historical significance above and beyond her role as a disturber of world peace. First, the recent history of Japan holds many lessons for the underdeveloped nations of the world. Starting in circumstances much like theirs, Japan accomplished the task each of them now faces: the creation of a modern state and a modern economy. Second, Japan has been the object of a great experiment in social change—the American Occupation. The successes and failures of the Occupation will be, when they are fully understood, a valuable guide to the limits of this type of cultural exchange.

I would like to express my grateful appreciation to the general editor of the Anvil series, Louis L. Snyder, for the innumerable ways in which he has aided in the preparation of the manuscript.

ARTHUR E. TIEDEMANN

TABLE OF CONTENTS

— 1 —

FROM SHOGUNATE TO NATIONAL STATE

The Land and the People. Japan, called by its inhabitants *Nihon* or *Nippon* ("origin of the sun"), is a chain of four large islands and innumerable small ones stretching along the coast of East Asia in a great 1500-mile arc that runs in a southeasterly direction from 45° to 30° north latitude. Its range of climate roughly parallels that of the eastern seaboard of the United States from Maine to Georgia, even to the extent of being subject to hurricanes (typhoons). Japan is mountainous; only about 16 per cent of its area can be used for agriculture. The only mineral present in any abundance is coal. There is much volcanic activity and the threat of earthquakes is always present. Japan has more than adequate precipitation, most places receiving between 60 and 100 inches annually. Japanese rivers, short and swift, are limited in their use for transportation, but ideal for hydroelectric power.

Japan has one mile of coast for every 8.4 square miles of area. This long, highly irregular coastline is bathed in the north by a cold current and in the south by a warm current. As a result the seas off Japan are rich fishing grounds, which play an important role in providing for the national diet. The land area of Japan is now 142,300 square miles: it is somewhat smaller than California (155,652), but larger than the British Isles (120,579). More than 50 per cent of the crop area is devoted to rice, the staple article of food. The other important crops are wheat, barley, naked barley, sweet potatoes, white potatoes, tea, and millet.

The basic Japanese ethnic stock is Mongoloid, to which have been added Malayan and Ainu strains. The Ainu, a proto-Caucasoid race, once inhabited the whole of Japan, but now there are only a few thousands of them left. At an early date these three races became well intermixed and the Japanese population is now fairly homogeneous. There is a wide range of physical types. However, the average Japanese is short—men averaging about five feet five inches. Generally, he has straight black hair, dark eyes, a dark complexion, fairly well-developed facial and body hair, an epicanthic fold which gives the appearance of slanted eyes, and a broad skull.

Though scholars are not yet in a position to generalize about Japanese national character, there are certain types of behavior that are prevalent in Japanese culture. The Japanese prefers to act as part of a group rather than as an individual. He has a high sense of loyalty to the group and tends to conform very closely to its standards. The family is important in Japan and frequently its pattern of organization is projected on to other groups. One of the most serious sanctions in the society is fear of bringing shame on the family. In weighty affairs a Japanese will use a go-between in order to avoid the possibility of any embarrassment which might arise in face-to-face relations. Suicide is an accepted form of protest or atonement, yet the suicide rate is much the same as that of Western countries.

The Japanese language is distantly related to Korean and the Altaic languages. For their writing system the Japanese use a combination of Chinese ideographs and phonetic symbols. This is necessitated by the structure of Japanese, which is inflected and polysyllabic.

The Origin of Military Rule. The early Japanese were organized socially and politically in a number of independent clans each ruled by an hereditary priest-chieftain. Toward the end of the first century after Christ, one of these clans began to establish a loose political and religious hegemony over the others. By the sixth century this clan had established its cult, that of the Sun Goddess, as the national religion. It had also gained the right to control foreign relations and thus to command any troops sent abroad. In addition, it was the arbiter in inter-clan disputes. Nevertheless, the clans still possessed a good deal of autonomy and the stronger among them competed with one another for control of the imperial clan. In the seventh century an effort was made to consolidate the authority of the central government by abolishing the clans and substituting for them a system of bureaucratic government and state ownership of the land modeled upon that of T'ang China.

Although all the outward forms of this system continued to exist, the hereditary principle soon reestablished itself and offices were distributed in accordance with it. Moreover, by a variety of techniques an increasing amount of land was removed from the government's tax registers. Throughout Japan there arose estates legally immune from both the fiscal and administrative authority of the local officials. Most of these properties were either owned by or under the protection of the great nobles of the imperial court. Gradually there developed a class of men who were employed by the great landholders to look after their interests in each locality. In the absence of a strong central government this often involved using force for the settlement of land disputes; hence these estate managers had to be adept in the use of arms. This was particularly true in eastern Honshu, where for a number of centuries the Japanese were engaged in subduing the original occupants of the islands, the Ainu. For their mutual protection the members of this evolving military class entered into pyramiding alliances with one another. By the middle of the twelfth century the heads of these various alliances were the *de facto* rulers in the provinces, although income from the land was still forwarded to the legal owners in the capital.

At this juncture the court nobles made the mistake of calling their adherents to the capital to help settle disputes which had broken out there. Before long, the warriors themselves assumed control over the exercise of the Emperor's powers. The various military factions fought with one another to determine which one would rule the nation. Out of this struggle Minamoto Yoritomo[1] and his followers emerged victorious. In 1192 the Em-

[1] Throughout the volume names are given in the Japanese fashion, surname first and praenomen second.

peror commissioned him *Seii-Tai-Shogun* (Barbarian-Sub-
duing-Generalissimo), with the right to nominate his own
successor. As Shogun, Yoritomo was commander-in-chief
of all the military forces and responsible for the internal
and external defense of the realm. Yoritomo's power was
grounded on the loyalty of several thousand trained
warriors, who managed lands scattered throughout Japan,
and who, because of their personal fidelity to him, were
ready to fight on his order. But there were many estates
held by people who did not have any personal tie to
the Shogun. To deal with this situation the Shogun secured imperial permission to establish on each estate a
steward whose duty it would be to collect a portion of
the estate rents as a tax for the support of the military
forces. In addition, a constable was appointed in each
province. This official was charged with maintaining order
in his province, and, to support his troops, he was allowed
to collect 1/50 of the annual rent of all the lands in the
province.

In 1333 the shogunate which Yoritomo had established
at Kamakura was brought to an end, largely as a result
of intrigues at the imperial court as well as growing
disaffection among the warrior class. A cadet branch of
the Minamoto family, the Ashikaga, obtained the title
of Shogun, but their authority never ran much beyond
the environs of Kyoto, the city which had long been the
imperial capital and now became the Shogun's seat. The
rest of Japan was parceled out among various local magnates over whom the Ashikaga had very little control.
Most of these men were descendants of the constables
whom the Kamakura shogunate had established in each
province. Since the constable's position was hereditary
and his power province-wide, the family which held this
office had been in a strategic position for asserting its
authority over the whole province. Once this had been
done, the more successful went on to seize adjacent
provinces. The domains of these magnates were not organized on the same model as European feudalism. Each
daimyo, as these men came to be called, collected taxes
from the cultivators of the land and used the proceeds
to pay his retainers. The organization was bureaucratic,
not feudal.

By the end of the fifteenth century, warfare among these princelings became endemic. The ambition of each magnate was to attain hegemony over all Japan. As the struggle wore on, many old families were extinguished and new *daimyo* arose from obscure origins. In the latter part of the sixteenth century, Oda Nobunaga went a long way toward unifying the country, but before he could complete the task he was struck down by an assassin. The power he had built up was seized by his ablest general, Toyotomi Hideyoshi, a farmer's son, who had started his career as a common foot soldier. By 1590 the last holdouts among the *daimyo* submitted to Hideyoshi and he was master of Japan. Although the last Ashikaga Shogun died in 1597, the title was denied to Hideyoshi because by custom only a Minamoto could become Shogun. Hideyoshi died in 1598, leaving as his heir an infant son. Tokugawa Ieyasu, the *daimyo* who next to Hideyoshi controlled the largest domain, plainly indicated that he intended to succeed Hideyoshi. His opponents were crushed at the Battle of Sekigahara, October 21, 1600. The following year Ieyasu forced all the *daimyo* to acknowledge his power over them by requiring them to sign an oath of loyalty. In 1603 the Emperor made him Shogun, an office he was eligible to hold since the Tokugawa were a branch of the Minamoto. The last threat to the Tokugawa Shogunate was eliminated in 1615 when the great castle which Hideyoshi had built at Osaka was taken and Hideyoshi's heir committed suicide.

The Tokugawa Shogunate. The great task to which Ieyasu and his immediate successors devoted themselves was assuring the perpetuation of Tokugawa dominance. The material basis of their power lay in the Shogunal domain, which consisted of lands producing about 31 per cent of the country's rice. Another 10 per cent was in the hands of branch Tokugawa families, while about 23 per cent was held by the *fudai daimyo*, the lords whom the Tokugawa especially trusted because they had submitted before the Battle of Sekigahara. The remaining lands, about 36 per cent, belonged to the *tozama daimyo*, the lords who had yielded only after Sekigahara. The Shogun-ate also controlled the gold and silver mines, and the im-

portant urban centers. Since the Emperor was the source
of all legitimate authority, the *daimyo* were denied access
to him and he was kept under the watchful eye of a Tokugawa governor. The *daimyo* were all compelled to
spend several months of the year in Edo, the Tokugawa
capital; whenever they returned to their domains, they
had to leave their wives and children as hostages. No
daimyo could, without the Shogun's consent, leave his
domain or contract a marriage. Nor could he coin money,
build warships, nor, except in certain specific instances,
move his troops beyond his borders. He might have
a castle only in his domainal capital, but the plans of
this castle had to be filed with the Shogunate. To prevent the *tozama daimyo* from undermining the Tokugawa from within, they were excluded from offices in
the central government. No taxes were collected from
the *daimyo,* but to hobble them financially the Shogunate
frequently imposed expensive special tasks on them.

The Tokugawa Class Structure. As part of their
effort to prevent any change which might undermine their
rule, the Tokugawa created a rigid, hereditary class structure. The highest class were the *samurai,* who constituted
about 6 per cent of the population. To this class belonged
all the military men from the Shogun to the lowest foot
soldier. They lived mostly in Edo or in the capitals of
the various *daimyo.* They were not allowed to practice
agriculture or to engage in a trade or craft. The income
on which they lived was derived from a rice allowance
made to them by their *daimyo.* The exact size of the
allotment depended upon the administrative or military
office held and might range from as high as 10,000 *koku*
of rice to as low as 20 *koku.* (A *koku* equals 4.96
bushels and is considered by the Japanese to be sufficient
to feed a person for one year.) In most domains the
various offices tended to become hereditary. With the
coming of peace the *samurai* who were not involved in
administration were reduced to idleness. To offset this the
Tokugawa deliberately encouraged the *samurai* to engage
in scholarly pursuits. As a result the military class also
became the intellectual class.

The vast majority of Japanese belonged to the second
ranking class, the farmers. Scholars at one time thought

that the Tokugawa village consisted of a number of small holders each having approximately the same amount of land. Recent research has completely changed this picture and conclusively shows that there were both landholders and tenants in the village. Tenancy varied in different parts of the country from 25 to more than 50 per cent. Among the landholders themselves there was a wide range in size of holdings: some having only an acre and a quarter, others having as many as 85 acres. The village more or less ran its own affairs, the lord of the domain generally having only a veto right in the election of the village officers. However, it was only the landholders who had the privilege of participating in the management of the village or of sharing in the common lands and water rights. The richer of these villagers were generally well educated and capable of keeping complicated official records. Technically, the landholder did not own the land, which was legally the Emperor's, but held the right of cultivation. Since this right was indefeasible and could be inherited, bought, or sold, it was, for all intents and purposes, ownership. All the landholders in the village were collectively responsible for the taxes levied on the village by the *daimyo*.

The last two classes recognized by the Tokugawa were, in order of rank, the artisans and the merchants. For convenience, they may be lumped together under the heading of townspeople. This group rose to great prominence during the Tokugawa period. At Edo, the Shogunal court and the large establishments which the hostage system required all the *daimyo* to maintain created an excellent market for the goods and services of townspeople. The Shogunate prohibited any direct trading between the various domains, and yet the *daimyo* was under the absolute necessity of selling his rice surplus in order to obtain funds for traveling to Edo and for supporting himself and his retinue there. The result was the creation at Osaka of a great buying-and-selling center. The large commercial population that grew up in Edo and Osaka generated its own cultural forms, such as the *Kabuki* drama, the woodblock print, and the novel of high life. As the wealth of the country flowed into their hands, they evaded the Tokugawa sumptuary laws and spent their money on lavish living. For instance, when they were forbidden to wear silk garments, they circumvented the prohibition by wearing ordinary cotton garments but lining them with colorful and expensive silks. Before long they had become the pacesetters for the *daimyo* and the *samurai*.

The Seclusion Policy. In 1639 the Tokugawa closed their country to all foreigners except the Dutch and the Chinese, who were permitted to trade at Nagasaki but only under the closest supervision. Three years earlier, an edict had been issued prohibiting, under pain of death, any Japanese from going abroad. (*See Reading No. 1.*) These two orders had an incalculable effect upon Japan's development: the one broke contact with the West just when Europe was about to make immense advances in civilization, and the other cut short a brilliant period of Japanese maritime expansion into East and Southeast Asia.

Once again the motive seems to have been the desire to avoid any threat to the stability of the regime. It was feared that Christianity, which had gained a substantial number of converts in Japan after the arrival of the first Westerners in 1542, would create a divided loyalty. There were also suspicions that the Christian Church was the advance guard of foreign invasion. For a number of years the Tokugawa tried to suppress Christianity without interfering with Western trade, but it seemed impossible for Portuguese ship captains to resist smuggling missionaries into the country. Consequently, the decision was made to end trade with all Westerners except the Dutch, who seemed to have no desire to proselytize. Another factor involved in this decision was concern lest the dispossessed *samurai* (*rōnin*) who had fled abroad when their lords were deprived of their domains should launch an attack on Japan. This fear was intensified by the poor performance of the troops sent to suppress the revolt of the Christian peasants at Shimabara (Kyushu) 1637-38. In 1640 a Portuguese embassy was sent from Macao to ask for a reopening of trade, but the Japanese refused and emphasized their determination to be rid of Portuguese traders by executing sixty-one members of the party.

Factors Undermining the Tokugawa Regime. The Shogunate was not able to prevent change. Economic and intellectual developments came about which were responsible eventually for toppling the regime. Paradoxically, for the economic difficulties which began to plague them from the early eighteenth century on, the Tokugawa had no one to blame but themselves. It was their own measures that had helped to bring a large merchant class into existence and had put that class in a position to profit from the *daimyo*. The establishment of peace after two centuries of constant warfare created in the seventeenth century a period of economic expansion and prosperity. By the end of the century the population was pressing up to the limit of the country's resources, given the existing technology. The condition of the agricultural producers worsened and it became difficult for the Shogunate and the *daimyo* to maintain their revenues. Yet, they and the *samurai* had become accustomed to a higher standard of living and now found it impossible to give it up. Consequently, the peasant was subjected to greater exactions and his condition was further reduced. Agrarian uprisings occurred with increasing frequency during the eighteenth and nineteenth centuries.

To meet its financial difficulties the Shogunate began to make forced loans from the merchants. It also adopted debasement of the coinage as a permanent part of the revenue system, thus creating inflation. These two expedients were not available to the ordinary *daimyo,* who soon fell hopelessly in debt. In an attempt to secure additional income, many of the *daimyo* established monopolies within their domains on various local products. Both they and the Shogunate also cut down the stipends of their *samurai,* who then had to turn to the moneylenders. So serious did this burden of debt become that the Shogunate on several occasions issued Acts of Grace relieving the *samurai* of the necessity of repaying loans made before a certain date, but after each such decree the debts soon piled up again. Profiting from all this, the merchants began to raise their status by buying adoption into *samurai* families or marrying their daughters to *samurai*. They also began, through various subterfuges, to gain control of farm lands and subject the peasant to an illegal rent. By the nineteenth century class lines had become blurred.

When the Tokugawa had first come to power, they tried to create an ideological basis for their regime by fostering the study of the Chu Hsi school of Confucianism. They were particularly attracted to this school by its stress on the virtues of filial piety and loyalty. Before long, however, schools of thought not so favorable to the Tokugawa came into existence. The first of these arose around a great project for research into early Japanese history sponsored by the *Daimyo* of Mito, a branch of the Tokugawa family. The scholars engaged in this work soon came to a true understanding of the legitimate position of the Emperor and in time became advocates of his restoration. The activities of these scholars were supplemented by the work of another group known as the School of National Learning. This school, originally interested in ancient Japanese poetry, had sought to recover the old Japanese language. This had led it to an investigation of the earliest examples of the Japanese language, the ancient historical chronicles. Since these chronicles had been designed in their day as propaganda for the imperial family and as a vehicle of nationalist feeling, it is not surprising that these latter-day students became rabid exponents of the virtues of national institutions, particularly the imperial family and the Shinto religion.

In 1630 the Shogunate banned the importation of any foreign book mentioning Christianity or written by a Jesuit. So zealously was this ban enforced that few foreign books found their way into the country. The Shogun Yoshimune (1716-44), recognizing that Japan was being deprived of valuable knowledge, in 1719 specifically authorized the importation of scientific works. In 1741 the same Shogun ordered two scholars to study Dutch, but not until the last quarter of the century did a knowledge of the Dutch language become widespread. Eager *samurai* threw themselves into its study in order to gain a first-hand knowledge of Western techniques in medicine, astronomy, surveying, armaments, military drill and tactics, cartography, and painting. In 1803 the Shogunate established a bureau for the translation of Dutch scientific works. As a result of these activities, long before Perry appeared, a large section of the *samurai* had obtained a substantial grasp of Western knowledge and were growing increasingly impatient with any attempt to restrict their studies.

The End of Seclusion. In the late eighteenth century informed Japanese were becoming increasingly concerned with Russian activities in Kamchatka, the Kuriles, and Sakhalin. Russian forces in that area were actually in no position to threaten Japan's security, but the imagined threat did point up the lack of sea and coastal defenses. In 1792 a Russian ship under the command of Lieutenant Adam Laxman came to Hokkaido to return some Japanese castaways and to ask for trading rights. He was thanked and given permission to go to Nagasaki for negotiations. The account of the experiences which the leader of the castaways had in St. Petersburg so impressed the ruling circles that Matsudaira Sadanobu, the chief minister, was converted to a trade policy. Unfortunately, Laxman never showed up at Nagasaki. By the time the next Russian mission appeared there in 1804, the climate of opinion was changed and the Russians were treated with hostility.

In the early nineteenth century the question of Japan's seclusion became of importance to the Western maritime nations, particularly to the United States. The ships carrying on the fur trade between the Pacific Northwest and China sailed past the Japanese archipelago. This was also true of the vast fleet of ships engaged in the whaling industry. There was always the danger of shipwreck on the Japanese coast and the attitude of the Japanese toward the luckless sailors left much to be desired. Even if no disaster befell a ship, the long voyage would be more bearable if Japan were available as a source of fresh food and water. Toward the middle of the century the introduction of the steamship complicated the problem by creating the need for coaling stations. Through the Dutch the Japanese kept an anxious eye on the international situation. The Shogunate was determined to keep the country closed, but it was sufficiently impressed with the defeat of China in the First Anglo-Chinese War to modify in 1842 its former shoot-on-sight order and at least permit foreign ships to take on water and supplies.

Discussions of the necessity for opening Japan began among American officials as early as 1815. There were several private attempts to deal with the Japanese, but none of the official plans was ever implemented until Commodore Biddle visited Edo Bay in 1846. This mission ended in failure, largely because the Japanese interpreted the Commodore's politeness as weakness. The indignities and dangers to which shipwrecked sailors were subjected, the ambitions of businessmen for commercial expansion in the Pacific, the strategic needs of the Navy, and the hope of missionaries for a harvest of souls finally determined the American government to deal firmly with the situation. On July 8, 1853, a strong squadron of American warships under the command of Commodore Matthew Calbraith Perry cast anchor in Edo Bay. Accompanied by an impressive military guard, Perry landed and delivered a letter from President Fillmore asking for trading privileges, coaling stations, and protection for shipwrecked Americans. Within a week he sailed away promising to return for an answer the following spring with an increased force.

Although the Shogunate had been warned about the American expedition by the Dutch, the actual appearance of Perry caused considerable consternation. The government was so unsure of itself that it took the unprecedented step of translating Fillmore's letter and sending it to the *daimyo* with a request for their advice. Of the 59 replies which are still extant, 25 favored opening the country to foreign trade, 19 did not relish foreign trade but counseled the avoidance of war, and only 15 suggested that Perry be categorically refused. Although this cross section represents only 20 per cent of the *daimyo,* it is indicative of the final decision arrived at by the Shogunate: all possible resistance short of war. When Perry returned in February, 1854, and made it clear that the issue was a treaty or war, the Japanese negotiators yielded and on March 31, 1854 signed the Treaty of Kanagawa. The terms opened Shimoda, a small fishing port southwest of Tokyo, and Hakodate in Hokkaido to American ships wanting to replenish their supplies, established the most-favored-nation principle, and provided for an American consul at Shimoda. Having yielded to the Americans, the Shogunate went on to sign similar agreements with the English (October 14, 1854) and the Russians (February 7, 1855), both of whom had fleets in Japanese waters.

As soon as it became apparent that a treaty was to be signed, relations between the members of the Perry mission and the Japanese negotiators, which had been strained, became more friendly and relaxed. Japanese visitors swarmed over the ships, eagerly examining every last piece of equipment. At dinner parties the Japanese were introduced to the mysteries of Western food and drink, and on one merry evening they went home in a high state of exuberance. On one occasion the Japanese guests were entertained with an impromptu American minstrel show, a courtesy they returned with a display of *sumo* (native Japanese wrestling). In the exchange of gifts which accompanied the festivities, the Americans were somewhat disappointed. The Japanese, however, were delighted with the rifles, revolvers, swords, liquors, and telegraph apparatus they were given. The gift which intrigued them the most was a complete miniature railroad—staid officials, their skirts flying, went whizzing around the Lilliputian tracks at twenty miles an hour. Despite the friendly manner of the Japanese negotiators, the foreigners were kept under close surveillance in order to prevent contacts between them and the ordinary Japanese. The fears of the authorities were well-founded, for on dark nights young *samurai,* thirsting for Western learning, would row out to the anchored ships and beg to be taken to America, a request which the Commodore felt constrained by the laws of hospitality to refuse. Whenever these violators of the seclusion edict were detected, they were executed. The willingness of these young men to risk death for a chance to gain knowledge of the outside world clearly shows that there were forces at work within Japan which, even if Perry or some other foreigner had never put in an appearance, would have eventually blown the doors open from the inside.

In August, 1856, Townsend Harris appeared at Shimoda as the first American Consul. By June, 1857, he succeeded in negotiating a convention which gave Ameri-

can citizens residence rights at Shimoda and Hakodate,
trading rights at Nagasaki, and extraterritoriality. He
continued to press for a more comprehensive treaty,
urging the danger that Japan would face when the French
and English finished their war in China and turned to
Japan. A draft treaty was agreed on in February, 1858.
This permitted the United States to station a minister in
Edo and consuls in all open ports. Edo and four other
ports were to be opened, and the U.S. Navy was allowed
to establish supply depots in Yokohama, Hakodate, and
Nagasaki. The Shogunate anticipated great opposition to
the treaty from the *daimyo*. Consequently, it decided
to delay signing it until the Emperor's approval was obtained. It was thought this would be a mere formality,
but as a result of the intrigues of certain court nobles
the Emperor refused his consent. In July, 1858, the Shogunate, anticipating the imminent arrival of the British,
finally signed the treaty anyway. By August the British
arrived and obtained a similar treaty. Then, in October,
another was signed with the French.

The Fall of the Shogunate. The signing of these
treaties was the signal for an outbreak of anti-Shogunate
and anti-foreign feeling. Dissident *daimyo,* in violation
of standing Tokugawa orders, flocked to the imperial
court. Ii Naosuke, the Shogun's chief minister, acted resolutely and even had the temerity to place the ringleader,
the Tokugawa *Daimyo* of Mito, under house arrest. As
a result, Ii Naosuke was assassinated by Mito men in
March, 1860. Meanwhile, attacks were being made on
foreigners by xenophobic *samurai,* who used as their
slogan the expression, "Honor the Emperor! Expel the
barbarians!" Harris's interpreter was killed in 1861.
Twice in that year the British legation was burned. In
1862 an Englishman, C. L. Richardson, was cut down
by the retinue of the *Daimyo* of Satsuma. In 1863 the
U.S. legation was burned and the American minister
followed the example of the rest of his colleagues and
withdrew to Yokohama. The Emperor summoned the
Shogun to Kyoto and kept him tarrying there from March
to July, 1863. Many of the *daimyo* were also gathered
there, for in October, 1862, the Shogunate had weakened
its hold on them by virtually abolishing the hostage sys-

tem. While at Kyoto the Shogun was forced to cons
to an imperial order to drive the foreigners out of th
country on June 25, 1863. However, the only one who
tried to obey this order was the *Daimyo* of Choshu, who
ordered his forts to fire on ships passing through the
Straits of Shimonoseki.

This was too much for the foreign representatives. They
decided to strike directly at the domains which had
offended them. In August, 1863, a British squadron
steamed into Kagoshima Bay and bombarded Kagoshima
city, the capital of Satsuma. In September, 1864, an allied
fleet leveled the Choshu forts. These lessons of Western
material strength were not wasted on Choshu and Satsuma; from this time on they stressed a policy of Westernization, particularly in military matters. Meanwhile, the
Shogun's position had been deteriorating. In early 1864
he was again summoned to Kyoto and was obliged to
agree that in the future the Emperor would invest the
daimyo with their domains. In addition, certain *daimyo*—
Satsuma, Choshu, Echizen, among others—were to be
allowed to act as imperial advisers. At this juncture the
Choshu men suddenly tried to kidnap the Emperor in
order to become the spokesmen of his will. They were
driven from Kyoto and the Shogun was ordered to punish them. It took him until July, 1866, before he could
gather an army to march on Choshu, and then his levies
were completely routed by the Westernized Choshu
troops. A month later the Shogun died. Since he was
childless, he was succeeded by a member of the pro-
imperial Mito branch of the Tokugawa. Beset with
problems of finance, foreign relations, and internal revolt,
his authority over the imperial court and the *daimyo*
dissipated, the new Shogun finally, on November 9, 1867,
submitted his resignation as Shogun to the young Emperor
Meiji, who had ascended the throne February 3, 1867.
This event began the Meiji Restoration.

The New Government.   Early in January, 1868, the
Emperor notified the ex-Shogun that direct imperial rule
had been reestablished and, at the same time, ordered him
to surrender his holdings. The followers of the Tokugawa
rose in rebellion against this demand, but were firmly
dealt with by the new rulers. Although scattered pockets

resistance continued to exist for more than a year, the important parts of the country were pacified by the fall of 1868, and the new government was soon able to turn its attention to the problem of devising a central administration.

The first few years saw numerous changes in the administrative structure. The senior offices with prestige were invariably divided among the court nobles and the *daimyo,* while the junior offices which involved the actual exercise of power were filled by an ambitious and highly capable group of younger *samurai*—such as Okubo Toshimichi, Kido Takayoshi, Goto Shojiro, Itagaki Taisuke, Soejima Taneomi, Saigo Takamori, Ito Hirobumi, Okuma Shigenobu, Yamagata Aritomo, Eto Shimpei and Inoue Kaoru. Most of these key men came from one or another of the four *tozama* domains which had played a major role in bringing down the Tokugawa—Satsuma, Choshu, Tosa, and Hizen. Though their rank was low, they had great influence in their domains and were the real leaders of the anti-Tokugawa movement. However, they still needed the cover of great names; not until the early 1870's did they themselves begin to occupy the top offices.

On April 6, 1868, before an assemblage of court nobles, *daimyo,* and *samurai,* the Emperor took a Charter Oath. (*See Reading No. 2.*) There were two significant aspects to the oath. First, it plainly indicated that the new government intended to embark upon a program of Westernization and that, by implication, anti-foreignism would no longer be tolerated. In point of fact, ruthless measures were taken to make the foreigners safe from attacks by murderous *samurai.* Second, the oath contained a promise of a deliberative assembly. This had been inserted to prevent unrest among the *samurai* of the various domains by assuring them that they were to have some voice in the government. An assembly of domain representatives was soon established, but it had little effect upon affairs and was abolished in 1873. However, in subsequent years this clause of the Charter Oath was exploited for their own purposes by those advocating a popular elective asembly.

The Abolition of the Daimyo Domains. In 1868 the central government had under its administrative and fiscal control only the former Tokugawa holdings. It first task was, therefore, to spread its authority to the *daimyo* domains. In March, 1869, the *daimyo* of Satsuma, Choshu, Tosa, and Hizen were persuaded to surrender their land registers. In July all *daimyo* who had not yet voluntarily done so were ordered to follow this precedent. To ease the transition the *daimyo* were retained as governors of their former domains at a salary equal to half their old revenues. Their *samurai* were also provided with pensions. Early in 1871, the government obtained contributions of troops from Satsuma and other domains. With this force to suppress any resistance, it then proceeded in August, 1871, to abolish the old domains and to replace them with prefectures administered by central government appointees. The *daimyo* and their families were ordered to reside in Edo, which had been made the capital and renamed Tokyo.

The Reforms of the Government. Early in the regime several decrees were issued abolishing the social restrictions which the Tokugawa had enforced. The road barriers were eliminated and freedom of movement was assured. Everyone was given the right to choose his own occupation. The farmer was allowed to plant what crops he would. The *samurai* lost his right of vendetta. The Tokugawa class system was completely eliminated. All Japanese were divided into three classes: the *daimyo* and the court nobles became the nobility (*kazoku*); *samurai* above the very lowest rank, gentry (*shizoku*); low-ranking *samurai* and all others, commoners (*heimin*).

Although this concession to pride of class was made, equality before the law was guaranteed to all. The abolition of the former military class made it necessary for the new rulers to develop their own armed forces. For the first few years they relied upon troops lent by the Satsuma, Choshu, and Tosa domains, but, in 1873, a conscription system modeled on that of Germany was instituted. All males over twenty were liable to three years of service. The French military mission, which originally helped to organize the new army, was later replaced with German advisers. A small navy was brought into being under the guidance of the English.

The Government recognized that the foundation of a

modern state was a literate citizenry. Therefore, in 1871, a Department of Education was established and commissioned to create an educational system. The new ministry had to start from scratch, for during the Tokugawa period there had been no public education. Since the new primary school system was modeled on the French system, it was highly centralized. Every child was obliged to finish three years of schooling, but some years passed before most of the eligible children were actually in attendance. Higher technical schools for medicine, navigation, agriculture, commerce, and fisheries were also soon in operation. A university system for more advanced professional training, inaugurated in 1871, was given its final organization in 1886. The initiative in this field was not left entirely to the State. Private universities were also founded: Keio as early as 1863; Doshisha in 1875; and Waseda in 1882. In its early years there was an extensive American influence in the school system. However, in the 1880's, German practices gained the ascendancy. Mori Arinori, the Education Minister from 1885 to 1889, frankly asserted that education was for the sake not of the individual but of the State.

State and Religion. The Shinto revival which occurred in the Tokugawa period, by its emphasis on the Emperor's divine right to rule Japan, provided the ideological justification for the Shogunate's overthrow. It is not surprising, therefore, to find the Meiji statesmen seizing upon Shinto as an excellent device for focusing the loyalty of the Japanese people upon the Emperor and his government. Shinto had originally been a somewhat primitive combination of nature- and ancestor-worship. It later developed a cosmology and a theogony which explained how Izanagi, the Sky-Father, and Izanami, the Earth-Mother, gave birth to the islands of Japan and to innumerable gods and goddesses; how one of their children, Amaterasu Omikami, became the Sun Goddess; and how the latter sent down her grandson to found a dynasty which was to rule over Japan forever. After the introduction of Buddhism in the sixth century after Christ, Shinto went more or less into eclipse, often its very shrines being administered by Buddhist priests, who identified the Shinto deity concerned with one or another manifestation of Buddhist divinities. But it never completely died out and the major shrines continued to be officially supported. Then, in the late Tokugawa period, a substantial recovery was made, and in addition to the intellectual revival already mentioned, there were founded many popular Shinto sects, each with its own special divinities and prescribed creed.

To be useful as a state cult, Shinto had to be divorced from its Buddhist and sectarian accretions. A first step, of course, was the careful separation of the popular Shinto sects, of which there are about thirteen major ones, from State Shinto. Only the latter was allowed to have shrines (*jinja*) where gods dwelled. Almost from the moment it assumed power the Meiji Government displayed an anti-Buddhist bias. Members of the imperial family were withdrawn from Buddhist orders and Buddhist ceremonies were forbidden within the palace. The old system of dual shrines was abolished and much Buddhist property was confiscated. In some localities mobs attacked and destroyed Buddhist temples. By 1872 the Government became convinced that Buddhism was too entangled with Shinto in the average Japanese's mind for the one to be attacked without harming the other; it, therefore, dropped its hostility. The Government's attitude toward Christianity was initially just as hostile and it continued the Tokugawa policy of suppression. When it became evident that this attitude was detrimental to the nation's foreign relations, the four thousand Christians held in prison were released and the anti-Christian edicts were allowed to die a quiet death.

Although it ended its attempt to suppress other religions, the Government continued its efforts to establish a State cult. By the 1930's it was supporting over 15,000 priests and more than 100,000 shrines. These shrines were organized in twelve grades, culminating in the Grand shrine at Ise, which was dedicated to the Sun Goddess. Attendance at these shrines was a test of loyalty for every Japanese, be he Shintoist, Buddhist, or Christian. The educational system and other propaganda media were used to indoctrinate Japanese with the three basic tenets of the cult: (1) that, as D. C. Holtom puts it, "The Emperor is divine because he is the extension in time of the very bodies and souls of the great divine ancestors of the past and, in particular, of the physical and spiritual attributes of the Sun Goddess . . ."; (2) that Japan is under the special guardianship of the gods and, therefore, its soil, its people, and its institutions are unique and superior to all others; (3) that it is Japan's divine mission to bring "the whole world under one roof" (*hakko ichi-u*) and thus extend to the rest of humanity the advantages of being ruled by the Emperor. As early as 1869, the Government initiated the policy of deifying and enshrining in Yasukuni Jinja the souls of those who died in the cause of the Emperor.

The Land Tax. When the Meiji Government assumed control of the *daimyo* domains, it continued to collect the traditional rice tax. This tied the Government's revenue to the fluctuations of the rice price and made fiscal planning almost impossible. It was decided to end this situation by establishing a land tax collected in money. To do this it was necessary that some person be responsible for each piece of land. Therefore, in 1872, the Government issued certificates of land ownership (*chiken*) to those who could prove they held cultivation rights. In this way a system of private land ownership was established. By means of a formula based upon the value of the rice crop produced on the land over a period of years, a capital value was fixed for each parcel of land. A 3 per cent annual tax was then levied on this value. This tax was the new regime's financial mainstay. In the 1870's it constituted 80 per cent of the revenue and, even as late as 1890, 70 per cent.

Among the agricultural population there was much dissatisfaction with this change. Forests, meadows, and other lands, which had been used by the villagers in common, were now taken over by the State. The new rate of taxation took, in local and national taxes, 30 to 40 per cent of the farmer's crop, and in most regions the tax burden was higher than under the *daimyo*. Moreover, the tax had to be paid in money at a definite time. This obliged the farmer to sell his crop as soon as possible and placed the burden of rice price fluctuations on him. The farmers were also annoyed by other Governmental innovations, such as the raising of the Eta and the Hinin, formerly social outcaste groups, to the level of ordinary citizens. They disliked the new conscription system and took literally the term "blood tax" which the Government applied to it. They were also unhappy about the taxes required to support the new primary school system. The outcome was a series of peasant rebellions in the early 1870's. These dwindled toward the end of the decade when inflation brought high rice prices and the Government cut the land tax to 2½ per cent, agreeing to accept part of it in kind.

The Crisis of 1873. Unrest was not confined to the farmers. Many of the *samurai* were beginning to feel that there was little place for them in the new order being created by the men who controlled the Government. Some of them had been absorbed into the growing apparatus of the State—the bureaucracy, the police, the military forces. Some had even managed to launch prospering business careers. But many could not make the change and longed for a return to the time when *samurai* were valued. This division of thought was also present in the *samurai* who composed the Government. Some, especially Kido, Okubo, Okuma, Ito, and Yamagata, submerged their loyalty to their fellow *samurai* into a larger loyalty to the State and felt that the ends of the State required the elimination of their old class. Others, including Saigo Takamori, Eto, Soejima, Goto, and Itagaki, believed that the *samurai* were still the backbone of the country and something must be done to save them. These two groups were somewhat evenly matched in numbers, but the votes of the two court nobles who were prominent in the Government, Sanjo Saneyoshi and Iwakura Tomomi, generally weighed the scales in favor of the former.

This balance was disturbed in October, 1871, when some of the more enthusiastic innovators—Ito, Okubo, and Kido—accompanied Iwakura on an embassy to Europe and the United States. Ostensibly the purpose of the trip was to secure a revision of the unequal treaties Japan had entered into under the Tokugawa, but the primary purpose was to learn as much as possible about Western technology and institutions with a view to further changes in Japan. The members of the mission tried to prevent an undoing of their work at home dur-

ing their absence by entering into a detailed written
agreement with those leaders who remained in Japan
precluding any basic change without their consent.
Nevertheless, Saigo Takamori and others, concerned over
the growing distress of the *samurai*, decided that a war
was necessary to restore the *samurai* to their proper
positions. The initial victim was to be Korea, which had
rejected several Japanese overtures for a treaty and con-
veniently produced several anti-Japanese incidents, but
the ultimate goal was to be China. Alarmed by reports
of what was happening at home, the chief members of
the Iwakura mission hastened to return. At Government
conferences held in October, 1873, they fought vigorously
against the war. They raised no objection to the idea of
expansion itself, but argued that Japan had to devote its
energies to achieving internal reform. Only when that
had been accomplished would the country be able suc-
cessfully to engage in foreign adventures. After a stormy
debate, the issue went against Saigo and his war program.
He and others who thought like him—Eto, Goto, Soejima,
and Itagaki—resigned from the Government in disgust.

Saigo returned to his native Kagoshima prefecture and
busied himself setting up private "schools" to indoctrinate
his fellow Satsuma *samurai* with his views. Others reacted
with more immediate violence. In January an assassination attempt was made on Iwakura, and the following
month in Saga prefecture Eto led 2,500 followers in an
armed revolt. The uprising was suppressed, but in order
to relieve the pressure the Government authorized Saigo
Takamori's brother, Saigo Tsugumichi, to lead a *samurai*
expedition to Formosa to punish the natives for killing
some Okinawan sailors. This created difficulties with
China which were finally resolved when China acknowledged the propriety of Japan's action and paid an indemnity.

The expedition did little to placate the disgruntled
samurai, since the Government supplied them with fresh
grievances. The expense of paying the *samurai* the pensions that had been establishd in 1869 was proving too
much for the nation's finances. Consequently, in 1873 the
Government offered a plan for the voluntary commutation
of the pensions into a lump sum payment in the form of

interest-bearing bonds. In August, 1876, this commutation plan was made compulsory. This device not only relieved the treasury of substantial annual payments but also bound the interests of the bond-holders to the Government. Most of the former *daimyo* came off very well under the terms of the commutation, but the average *samurai* was virtually expropriated. In the fall of 1876 *samurai* revolts broke out in Kumamoto, Fukuoka, and Yamaguchi prefectures, but were quickly put down. The Government, worried over the possibility of revolt in Satsuma, decided to remove the stores of the Kagoshima City arsenal to a safe place. This preventive measure proved to be the tocsin for revolt in southern Kyushu: in January, 1877, Saigo Takamori took the field "to save the Emperor from evil counselors." This was the greatest test yet faced by the central Government. The new conscript army with its superior weapons and communications proved equal to its task. By September, 1877, Saigo was dead and the rebellion crushed.

The Beginnings of Political Parties. When Itagaki Taisuke withdrew from the Government in 1873, he decided to attack his former colleagues by political rather than military action. In January, 1874, he organized the first public political association in Japan, the *Aikoku Koto,* and shortly thereafter submitted a memorial asking for the establishment of a representative assembly. (*See Reading No. 3.*) Later he returned to his native prefecture, Kochi, and in April, 1874, established another political society called the *Risshisha.* This group not only advocated political reform but also tried to assist *samurai* in getting on their feet economically. In February, 1875, a meeting of representatives sent by the *Risshisha* and similar groups in other localities was held at Osaka and a national party, the *Aikokusha,* was formed. This collapsed the very same month when Itagaki was enticed back into the Government on the promise that some reforms would be made.

In October, 1875, Itagaki, dissatisfied with the failure to make any real change, again withdrew. The next few years witnessed an intensified propaganda campaign for a representative assembly. The ideas of Mill, Bentham, Rousseau, and Spencer had been made available in translation and were freely used in the anti-Government struggle. The main channel for this propaganda was a number of small newspapers. The Government, in its turn, subsidized newspapers and used the very severe Press Law of June, 1875, to suppress the opposition's voice. By 1878 the *Aikokusha* was resurrected, but this time, while the *samurai* still provided most of the leadership, an increasingly important role was taken by the landowning class, which resented the heavy taxation of its land and its small manufacturing enterprises. After the Satsuma Rebellion and the assassination of Okubo in 1878, the Government was in no mood for trifling. On the one hand, it gave certain concessions. In 1878 representative assemblies were established in each prefecture and given limited financial power. Two years later the same kind of assemblies were inaugurated in cities, towns, and villages. On the other hand, in April, 1880, it issued a set of regulations for public meetings and associations which made political activities very difficult and rendered it virtually impossible to have any national organizations.

The Promise of a Constitution. Although the Government high-handedly suppressed political agitation, it was not indifferent to the need for establishing a definitive political structure. For some time the higher officials had been discussing this matter. One of the leading members of the oligarchy, Okuma Shigenobu, was reticent about his views and did not submit his suggestions to the Emperor until March, 1881. In June, when the other members of the Government discovered the nature of his recommendations, they were thunderstruck. Okuma had proposed the establishment of a system quite like England's and the calling of a parliament by 1883. Nothing might have come of Okuma's plan but for another issue that arose at the same time. Late in July the Government decided to sell to an Osaka syndicate the enterprises that had been established in Hokkaido to aid colonization and economic development. Okuma's subordinates leaked this information to the press. Public fury was unbounded when it was discovered that the purchase price was only a small part of the amount originally invested and that among the purchasers were former employees of the development bureau. Serious disturbances broke out and the cry went up that a parliament was necessary to prevent political corruption. On the night of October 11, 1881, the Emperor presided over a meeting attended by all the members of the Government with the exception of Okuma, who was not invited. It was decided that the sale would be canceled, that Okuma would be dismissed, and that a parliament would be established in ten years. The following day an imperial rescript was issued promising the nation a parliament by 1890. (*See Reading No. 4.*)

Immediately thereafter Itagaki founded the *Jiyuto* (Liberal Party), and early the next year Okuma organized the *Kaishinto* (Progressive Party). To support its cause the Government arranged for its followers to establish the *Teiseito* (Imperial Rule Party). In June, 1882, the Government strengthened the regulations controlling meetings and associations. It also cleverly removed Itagaki from the scene by indirectly supplying him with funds for a trip abroad.

Meanwhile, the deflationary policy instituted in 1881 was creating distress in the countryside. This was intensified by a series of natural calamities. In an effort to relieve their condition the poorer farmers and tenant farmers used the local party branches for agitation against taxes and rent. In the mid-1880's a number of riots occurred in different sections of the country. Fearful of becoming involved in insurrection and unsympathetic to the radicals' economic demands anyway, the *Jiyuto* leaders dissolved their party and the *Kaishinto* suspended operations.

Foreign Relations. One of the early problems of Meiji foreign relations was the establishment of the boundaries of Japan. In the north the boundary was settled in 1875 by a treaty which awarded Sakhalin (Karafuto) to Russia and the Kuriles (Chishima) to Japan. In the same year the Powers recognized Japan's sovereignty over the Bonins (Ogasawara). In 1879 Japan established her direct government in Okinawa (Ryukyus) and, by 1881, obtained Chinese acceptance of this *fait accompli*. In 1871 Japan concluded a commercial treaty with China by which each country granted the other extraterritoriality but which had no most-favored-nation clause and, therefore, denied each the privileges the

Western Powers had obtained. It was not until 1876 that Japan was finally able to secure a commercial treaty with Korea. The treaty granted the Japanese extraterritoriality and provided for the opening of three ports.

While willing to exercise consular jurisdiction in Korea, the Japanese deeply resented the extraterritoriality enjoyed by Westerners within Japan. No less galling to them was the loss of tariff autonomy which had been occassioned by a treaty signed in 1866. Almost from the moment the Meiji Government came to power, it made every effort to procure a revision of the unequal treaties. In 1878 the United States signed a treaty surrendering its tariff privileges, but this agreement never went into effect since it was conditional upon similar treaties being concluded with all the Powers. During the first six months of 1882 Inoue Kaoru, the Foreign Minister, conducted an inconclusive series of conversations with foreign representatives in Tokyo. However, the Japanese were given to understand that extraterritoriality would be ended when their laws had achieved Western standards; this undoubtedly hastened the revision of the Japansese law codes. A new series of talks were held by Inoue in 1886-87. During this period the Japanese Government leaders went to great extremes in an effort to prove to the foreign negotiators that Japan was becoming Westernized. These negotiations came to an abrupt end when it leaked out that Inoue was prepared to open the whole country to foreign travel and establish joint foreign-Japanese courts to try cases involving foreigners. Inoue was forced to resign. The public mood became so nasty that in December, 1887, the Government issued a Peace Preservation Law empowering the police to deal summarily with secret societies, public meetings, instigators to riot, and the like. It also permitted the Home Minister to prohibit any suspected person from being within 7½ miles of the imperial palace. General Yamagata, the Home Minister, immediately banished some 300 people, including such prominent editors as Ozaki Yukio. To placate the public, Okuma was made Foreign Minister. He instituted a policy of negotiating with each nation separately and, at the same time, made life difficult for foreign residents. He managed to achieve a certain amount of success with

Mexico, the United States, Russia, and Germany, but England remained adamant until the eve of the Sino-Japanese War.

From this period may be dated a resurgence of anti-foreignism in Japan. Patriotic Japanese resented the implication that their laws and institutions were inferior to those of the West. Groups sprang up with the avowed aim of preserving the national culture. Sometimes they operated on the intellectual level. There was, for instance, a revival of interest in Confucian morality which eventually found expression in the Imperial Rescript on Education issued in 1890. (*See Reading No. 6.*) At other times they turned to direct action, as did the *Genyosha,* an ultra-nationalistic secret society founded by Toyama Mitsuru. It was a member of this society who on October 18, 1889, threw a bomb at Okuma and cost him one of his legs. It is indicative of the status enjoyed by Japanese political assassins that Okuma sent a money gift to his attempted killer's family and that in 1921 both Okuma and Toyama attended a ceremony commemorating the 33rd anniversary of the event.

Economic Changes in the Early Meiji Period. The Meiji leaders were desperately concerned with the preservation of Japan's independence. They were farsighted enough to see that the nation's military forces could not be very effective unless behind them there stood a modern economy capable of supplying their needs. The creation of this up-to-date economy was one of the main tasks these leaders set themselves. A beginning had already been made in the Tokugawa period by both the Shogunate and the *daimyo* domains. The Satsuma domain was a leader in this respect. Before 1860 it had established a reverberatory furnace, a shipbuilding yard, and an arsenal. By 1866 it had imported English cotton spinning machinery, along with technical instructors. At about the same time the Shogunate was making a beginning with what was to become the famous Yokosuka Naval Yard. The Meiji Government absorbed most of these plants and added strategic enterprises of its own. It also established a number of pilot plants in other fields—cotton spinning, silk reeling, tiles, cement, woolens, and bleaching powder. These were designed both to supply immediate needs and to serve as models for private entrepreneurs. In 1871 a postal and telegraph system was inaugurated. The next year the first railroad was completed and by 1893 the country had 2,000 miles of track. The Government also took the initiative in opening up mines. After 1880 it was decided that the State would withdraw from industrial and mining activities, so that most of these enterprises were sold to various favored private interests at extremely low prices. It was at this time that many of the *Zaibatsu* families laid the foundation for their future great wealth.

These economic activities created two problems for the Government: how to concentrate investment capital within the country and how to secure the foreign exchange necessary to finance a vast import of foreign equipment and technical assistance. Since its primary source of revenue was agriculture, it was largely by heavy taxation of this sector of the economy that industrial capital was secured. Imports were paid for by the export of agricultural products such as silk, tea, and rice, as well as by a limited amount of specie. This was all made possible by extraordinary increases in agricultural yields, which were achieved at relatively little cost by introducing improved seed strains, improving land use, bettering irrigation and drainage, etc. Thus between 1878-82 and 1888-92 the area under cultivation increased by 7 per cent and the yield went up by 21 per cent while the population only rose by about 15 per cent. This agricultural surplus was siphoned off not only by taxes but also by the postal savings system which was set up in 1875. In addition inflation, created by the Government's free use of the printing press, also acted as an invisible tax. The volume of currency was increased by the new National Banks, which were authorized to issue notes up to 80 per cent of their capital, this capital being largely in the form of pension commutation bonds. However, after 1881 a deflationary policy was instituted and a convertible currency issue, the responsibility of the newly created Bank of Japan (1882), was established. The one source of funds which the Government resolutely declined to avail itself of were foreign loans. Before 1895 it was feared that political strings would be attached to such loans, and hence only two small ones were made.

In 1894, although Japan had made substantial progress in industrialization, it was still basically an agricultural country. Farming was the occupation followed by 70 per cent of the households, and 84 per cent of the people lived in places under 10,000. There were only a little more than 200 steam-powered plants, fewer than 400,000 spindles, and fewer than 1,000 power looms. Almost no steel was produced and only 40 per cent of the pig iron requirements were met domestically. Foreign bottoms still carried about 90 per cent of the nation's foreign trade.

Promulgation of the Constitution. The task of preparing the constitution which the Emperor had promised was given to Ito Hirobumi. He spent the years 1881-83 in Europe studying Western constitutions. Upon his return to Japan, he began the actual task of drawing up the constitution. Soon he introduced preliminary changes in the governmental structure. In 1884 a peerage was created and ranks of nobility distributed to the old court nobles (*kuge*), the former *daimyo*, and the various Government leaders. Then, in 1885, the central administration was reorganized and a cabinet on the German model instituted, Ito becoming the first Prime Minister. By 1888 a draft of the constitution was ready and to review Ito's work a privy council was set up. After numerous discussions and some minor changes, this body gave its approval to his draft. Finally, on February 11, 1889, the Emperor, in a court ceremony, promulgated the document. For the first time the general public learned the nature of its provisions.

— 2 —

JAPAN BECOMES A WORLD POWER

The Meiji Constitution. The structure of the Japanese State was determined only in part by the Meiji Constitution. (*See Reading No. 7.*) For a full understanding a number of supplementary laws and decrees as well as extra-legal customs must also be taken into account. The emperor combined in his person all executive, legislative, and judicial powers, but he never exercised these powers except on advice. His primary political advisers were the Prime Minister and the other cabinet ministers, or what is commonly referred to as the Government. No signature of the Emperor on a political document was valid unless they countersigned it. In the exercise of one of his greatest powers, the appointment of the Prime Minister, the Emperor relied upon the counsel of the statesmen who had made the Restoration —Ito, Yamagata, Matsukata, Oyama, and Inoue, and later Kuroda, Katsura, and Saionji, a group known collectively as the *genro* (elder statesmen). Once the Prime Minister had been appointed, the Emperor accepted his recommendations for the other ministers. These men then had at their command all the Emperor's political powers.

The Meiji Constitution established certain restraints upon the use of these powers. By its terms, a Diet was established consisting of a House of Peers and a House of Representatives. In the House of Peers, there were certain peers who sat for life (princes, marquises); other peers were elected by their fellow peers for seven-year terms (counts, viscounts, barons). A second category of members consisted of imperial appointees, who served for life and were generally distinguished bureaucrats. In addition, the larger taxpayers in each prefecture were allowed to elect one or two seven-year-term members. This body was designed to serve as a conservative counterweight to the House of Representatives; it did not prove disappointing in this respect. The members of the House of Representatives were chosen by popular election, but the original Election Law established property qualifications for voting under which only about 450,000 persons were eligible.

The Diet's powers, in which both houses shared fully, were of two kinds: financial and legislative. The Government was required to present its plans for expenditure and revenue to the Diet annually in the form of a budget. No changes in tax rates could be made or new taxes established without the Diet's consent, nor could any loans be contracted. However, the Diet did not really possess that ultimate power of the purse which other legislatures have used so effectively to establish their control over the executive. The Government was allowed to issue emergency financial decrees if a need arose while the Diet was not in session. These were later submitted to the Diet, but, even if they were rejected, action taken under them was valid. Although there were several other limits on the Diet's financial control, the greatest one was contained in Article 71, which provided that, if the Diet failed to pass the budget, the current budget automatically would continue on into the next year. Thus the only real financial power the Diet possessed was merely the right to deny the Government an increase in funds.

The Diet's consent was also required for the enactment of a law, but here again there were substantial limitations. Matters which had to be dealt with in the form of law were more or less enumerated in the Constitution. Any other matter could be handled by Governmental decree. Among the most important of the enumerated matters were the rights guaranteed to Japanese subjects, all of which were qualified by the phrase "according to the provisions of law." Even the enumerated matters could be the subject of a decree if an emergency arose during the Diet's recess, although in this case the matter had to be submitted to the next Diet session. There were certain powers which were reserved to the Emperor and beyond the purview of the Diet. These included the conduct of diplomatic relations, declaration of war, making peace, determination of the structure of the executive, the pay of civil and military officials, granting of amnesties, pardons, and commutations, declaration of state of siege, introduction of constitutional amendments, the regulation of succession, and the establishment of a regency. The Emperor, that is, the Government, could also issue any orders necessary for carrying out the laws or required "for the maintenance of the public peace and order, and for the promotion of the welfare of the subjects." The functioning of the Diet was subject to the control of the Government, which had the power to convoke, prorogue, and dissolve it. Unless the Government called a special session or extended the ordinary session, the Diet met only once a year in a three-month session, actually only about two months since a month was taken up by the New Year's recess.

The best weapon of the Diet in its struggle with the Government was the right of interpellation, which might be used to take up almost any matter. Either house might also pass resolutions of censure or non-confidence, but these had no effect in law and the Diet never did succeed in establishing the principle of ministerial responsibility. Therefore, the only function such resolutions had was to arouse public opinion against the Government.

Another important part of the governmental structure was the Privy Council. This was established because it was too dangerous to allow all the vast powers of the Emperor to be exercised solely at the discretion of the Cabinet. This body had to approve constitutional amendments, laws and decrees supplementary to the Constitution, emergency decrees, emergency financial decrees, treaties, international agreements, and declarations of martial law. It consisted of a president, a vice-president and 24 councilors, as well as the cabinet ministers.

There was one power of the Emperor which was excluded from the competence of the cabinet ministers. This was the supreme command of the military forces. (*See Reading No. 5.*) In exercising his command of the military forces the Emperor's proper advisers were the Chief of the Army General Staff, the Chief of the Naval General Staff, the Army Minister, and the Navy Minister.

This system had begun with the establishment of the Army General Staff in 1878 and was explicitly recognized in the Cabinet Regulations of 1885 and 1889. Although it is not found in the Meiji Constitution, it cannot be considered to be extra-legal. The practice of restricting the Army and Navy Ministers to officers on the active list also goes back to pre-constitutional times. The existence of these two practices was responsible for the power of the military in the Japanese State, for the first permitted them to take action without securing Cabinet concurrence, and the second permitted them to wreck any Cabinet by declining to provide an Army or a Navy Minister or by withdrawing the same. Technically speaking, whenever the command function involved finances, the rights and obligations of citizens, or international relations, it was quite proper for the Cabinet to give advice.

The New System in Operation. On July 1, 1890, elections were held for the House of Representatives. In November of the same year the first session of the Diet was opened. The *Jiyuto* and the *Kaishinto* were reconstituted, but neither of these parties dominated the lower house since in the beginning the representatives tended to organize themselves into a number of fluid blocs. Because of the restricted electorate, the lower house represented primarily the propertied classes, particularly the agricultural landowners, whose main concern was to make the Government reduce its spending and cut taxes. The Government, on the other hand, was determined to obtain as much money as possible out of the Diet in order that its program of economic and military expansion might be carried forward. When the first budget was presented to the Diet, the lower house slashed it by more than 10 per cent. The Prime Minister, Yamagata, was annoyed but hesitated to create a bad impression by dissolving the very first Diet. In the end the Government managed to persuade a number of members to change their votes and some of the cut was restored.

In May, 1891, Matsukata, the Finance Minister, replaced Yamagata as Prime Minister. Matsukata presented an ambitious budget to the Second Diet, calling for naval expansion, the establishment of a steel works, and nationalization of the railroads. When his budget was rejected, he dissolved the lower house. In the election held in February, 1892, the Home Minister, determined to win at all costs, used both bribery and force extensively. A number of people were killed and many injured. There was widespread criticism even in Government circles, and the House of Peers passed a resolution censuring the Home Minister. When the Third Diet met in May, 1892, the lower house passed a non-confidence resolution. Matsukata ignored this, but finally resigned when the Army and Navy Ministers left the Cabinet because they resented the dismissal of the Home Minister.

The *genro* picked Ito to head the next cabinet. However, the author of the Constitution proved no better than his predecessors at the task of inducing the Diet to cooperate with the executive. The Fourth Diet, meeting in November, 1892, again delayed the budget and sent a memorial to the Throne censuring Ito. Ito promptly secured from the Emperor a message which not only rejected the memorial but announced to the Diet that the Emperor was making a personal donation to the naval fund and was ordering all officials to contribute one-tenth of their salaries. By this invocation of the Emperor's prestige, Ito obtained the immediate passage of the budget. At the next session of the Diet in November, 1893, there were two important events. First, public confidence in the Diet's integrity was shaken when Hoshi Toru, the president of the lower house, was expelled from the house for bribery connected with the establishment of the stock exchange. Second, when the lower house asked the Emperor to remove one of the Cabinet members, they were explicitly told that the appointment and dismissal of ministers was the Emperor's concern and not to be meddled in by them.

At this session the Diet found in the treaty revision issue a useful weapon with which to attack the Government. Since this was a patriotic issue, the Government found it difficult to deal with its critics. Ito, therefore, dissolved the Diet. Elections were held and the Sixth Diet met in May, 1894. The lower house immediately prepared to pass a resolution indicting the Government for its conduct of foreign relations; Ito again dissolved it. By the time new elections were held the Sino-Japanese War had broken out and the new Diet gave the Government everything it asked. Meanwhile, negotiations for the revision of the unequal treaties were meeting with success. On July 16, 1894, the Aoki-Kimberley Treaty was signed. Under its terms extraterritoriality was to be abolished in 1899 and tariff autonomy restored. Similar treaties were signed with the other nations involved, and by 1911 Japan had regained all its rights as a sovereign nation.

The Sino-Japanese War. By the early 1880's there was a Japanese legation in Korea and Japanese merchants were active in that country. Japan's policy at this time was to secure the recognition of Korean independence by all the powers concerned. She was especially anxious that China should not consider Korea as a tributary state. The Japanese Government felt that Korea in the hands of another power would be a serious military danger. Korea also seemed to be a natural field for the future expansion of Japanese interests and the Japanese did not wish to be forestalled in this matter. In Korean domestic affairs the Japanese Government usually took the side of those who wished to introduce Western reforms, for it seemed that only in this way could Korean independence be maintained. This support of the reformers naturally aroused the antagonism of Korean conservatives. In 1882 fighting broke out between the reformers and the conservatives. Chinese troops under Yuan Shih-k'ai restored order, but not before several Japanese officials were murdered. A Japanese expedition forced the Koreans to sign the Treaty of Chemulpo, under which Japan received the right to station troops to guard her legation. The Chinese, who were also given this privilege, from this time on began to reassert their suzerainty in Korea. In 1884 the reformers, with Japanese aid, seized the Korean king and set up a new government. China intervened and released him. For a time war was imminent, but Ito visited Li Hung-chang, the chief Chinese official, in Tientsin and they agreed upon a settlement. Both nations were to withdraw their troops within four months; neither was to dispatch troops to Korea without written notice; and the Korean army was to be trained by instructors from a third country.

Before long, Yuan Shih-k'ai, the Chinese Resident in Korea, managed to establish his dominance over the Korean Government. As a result the Japanese felt all their work had been undone. In June, 1894, a Korean religious sect rebelled, whereupon the Korean Government asked the Chinese to send in troops. When the Japanese also sent in troops, a crisis developed, neither side being willing to withdraw. On July 25, 1894, a flotilla of three Japanese warships came across a military transport, the *Kowshing,* on its way to Korea with reinforcements. The escorting vessels opened fire on the Japanese, and the Sino-Japanese War had begun.

The initial reaction of many foreign observers was that Japan was doomed to defeat in this struggle with her gigantic neighbor. They were mistaken. Japanese equipment and training were superior to those of China. Moreover, the Japanese were able to concentrate their forces much more effectively. The Japanese Navy met and drove from the sea the northern Chinese fleet, whose fighting power had been seriously reduced by the corruption of the Chinese Government. The Chinese were swept out of Korea. By November the Japanese were in Manchuria and had seized Port Arthur. In February, 1895, Wei-hai-wei, a port on the Shantung peninsula, which had been besieged by the Japanese, fell, and the Chinese fleet was captured.

In March, Li Hung-chang came to Japan as peace emissary and on April 17, 1895, the Treaty of Shimonoseki was signed. By its terms China recognized Korea's independence; ceded to Japan the island of Formosa, the Pescadores, and the Liaotung peninsula; and agreed to pay an indemnity of 200,000,000 taels. Japan was allowed to occupy Wei-hai-wei until the indemnity was paid and a suitable treaty of commerce signed. This last matter was important, for it resulted in the Sino-Japanese Commercial Treaty of 1896, a treaty that gave Japan the same privileges the Western powers enjoyed in China and, in addition, the right to operate factories in the treaty ports. But Japan was not to escape with all her loot. On April

23, 1895, Russia, France, and Germany presented her with identical notes "advising" her to return the Liaotung peninsula to China. It was plain that Russia would fight if the demand were not met. Japan, alone and in no condition to fight three major powers, yielded but received an additional 30,000,000 taels in indemnity.

Failure of the First Party Cabinet. When the war ended, Ito, who was still Prime Minister, exerted himself to secure party support. The *Jiyuto* responded to his overtures, and as a reward Itagaki, its leader, was taken into the Cabinet as Home Minister. When this appointment aroused strong criticism, Ito resigned, and in September, 1896, was succeeded by Matsukata. Recognizing that he must cooperate with the Diet, Matsukata appointed Okuma as Foreign Minister and gave several positions to members of Okuma's newly organized *Shimpoto* (Progressive Party). In January, 1897, after the chief cabinet secretary, a *Shimpoto* man, published an article criticizing the Imperial Household officials, the Government felt itself obliged to suspend his magazine. This incident estranged the *Shimpoto* from Matsukata. Consequently in November, just before the Eleventh Diet met, Okuma led his followers out of the Cabinet. The lower house, in solid opposition to the Government, passed a non-confidence resolution. Matsukata's reaction was to dissolve the Diet and then resign himself. Ito organized his third cabinet but could not entice either Okuma or Itagaki into it. When the new Diet met in May, 1898, it rejected the land-tax increase bill, a measure which was vital to the expansion of the nation's military establishment. Ito thereupon obtained a dissolution.

In June, 1898, the *Jiyuto* and the *Shimpoto*, the two major parties, amalgamated to form the *Kenseito*. About the same time, the *genro* were meeting to decide what to do about the impasse the Government's financial plans had reached. Yamagata thought the solution was to suspend the Constitution and eliminate the Diet's financial controls. Ito argued that there were only two paths open: either he should organize a political party or the *Kenseito* should be given the responsibility of government. When Yamagata and the other *genro* finally agreed to the second choice, the dazed leaders of the new party were asked to form a cabinet. Okuma became Prime Minister and Itagaki the Home Minister, the rest of the positions being parceled out between the two factions of the party. Bureaucrats were thrown out of their jobs and replaced with party worthies. Great plans were made for reorganizing the administrative structure and cutting costs. In the August Diet election the party won about 85 per cent of the seats. At this juncture the two factions fell out over the distribution of spoils, and the Cabinet had to resign in November, 1898.

Yamagata took advantage of Ito's absence in China to make himself Prime Minister. The old *Jiyuto* faction agreed to support Yamagata in return for the Government's sponsoring of bills to increase the salaries of Diet members, to lower the voting qualifications from 15 to 10 yen, and to establish the secret ballot. With the *Jiyuto* faction's support and whatever votes he could pick up by bribery or other forms of pressure, Yamagata obtained his increase in the land tax. He also issued civil service regulations which would effectively prevent any application of the spoils system to the bureaucracy. To prevent any future party cabinet from changing these regulations, he made the consent of the Privy Council a prerequisite to any alteration. As the creator of the modern Japanese Army, he was anxious to keep it free of party control too. Therefore, he rewrote into the law the provision that only active military officers might hold the two service ministries.

When Yamagata resigned in October, 1900, he was followed as Prime Minister by Ito, who had the previous month become president of a new political party, the *Seiyukai*. Despite the dictatorial terms on which he exercised his presidency, Ito attracted a huge majority of the lower house into the *Seiyukai*. He proceeded to organize a cabinet in which all the civilian ministers were party members. His large majority helped him to push his enormous budget through the lower house, but the House of Peers expressed its resentment against Ito's surrender to the party principle by voting the budget down. Ito was forced to secure an imperial rescript ordering the Peers to pass the measure. In May, 1901, a quarrel developed in the Cabinet over financial plans, and Ito resigned. A Yamagata protégé, General Katsura Taro, then became Prime Minister. The Katsura cabinet managed to stay in power until January, 1906. Katsura's main problem was obtaining approval by the Diet of the increasingly large military estimates. By a combination of blandishments, bribes, force, and dissolutions he generally succeeded in securing the approval, until the Russo-Japanese War relieved him of his Diet troubles.

War and Rapprochement with Russia, 1895-1914. The Sino-Japanese War had given Japan a paramount position in Korea, but this was lost late in 1895 when a Korean uprising, in which Japanese participated, led to the murder of the Korean queen. The king and the crown prince took refuge in the Russian embassy where they became subject to Russian influence. During the next few years the Japanese attempted to obtain Russian recognition of Japan's special position in Korea. Twice it seemed as if they had succeeded (Yamagata-Lobanov Agreement of June 5, 1896, and Nishi-Rosen Convention of April 28, 1898), but the Russians paid little regard to the arrangements. The crowning insult came in 1898 when Russia, during the scramble for concessions, secured a leasehold on the Liaotung peninsula and railroad concessions in Manchuria. Japan established a sphere of influence in Fukien province across from Formosa, but this did not compensate for the Liaotung injustice.

In 1899, when the Boxer Rebellion broke out in China, Japan sent troops to participate in the Allied Expedition to relieve the legations at Peking. The Japanese, behaving in an exemplary fashion, made a good impression upon foreign observers. However, the Boxer Rebellion brought fresh difficulties with Russia, which had poured troops into Manchuria and was badgering the Chinese to give her control of the area. Finally, in April, 1902, the Russians agreed under pressure from the various Powers to evacuate all troops within eighteen months. Meanwhile, common fear of Russia brought the Japanese and the English together, and on January 30, 1902, the Anglo-Japanese Alliance was signed. The terms of the treaty, which was to run for five years, recognized England's primary interest in China and Japan's in Korea. In effect, it provided that if, in the defense of its interests, one partner had to go to war with more than one country, the other partner would join in the war.

When the time limit for Russia's withdrawal expired, her troops were still in Manchuria. In June, 1903, the Japanese decided that they would yield Manchuria to Russia but that Korea must be Japanese. In August, 1903, the Japanese ambassador in Russia began negotiations toward this end. But the Russians were not willing to surrender Korea. The Japanese then decided that the only solution was war. Diplomatic relations were broken on February 7, 1904, and the next day Port Arthur was attacked.

On land and sea the Japanese were uniformly successful. By March, 1905, the Russian troops were cleared from southern Manchuria. In May, 1905, the last Russian fleet was destroyed in the Battle of Tsushima. Since the war, however, seriously strained Japan's material and human resources, the Portsmouth Peace Conference came as a welcome relief. The Portsmouth Treaty was signed on September 5, 1905. By its terms Russia recognized Japan's paramount interest in Korea; transferred her rights in Liaotung and the southern section of the Manchurian railroad to Japan; and ceded Sakhalin south of the 50th parallel. The Japanese negotiators desired to hold out for an indemnity, but the Japanese military leaders insisted that the war be terminated.

When the Anglo-Japanese Alliance was renewed in August, 1905, it dropped all reference to Korean independence and recognized Japan's right to control the country. In return, the scope of the alliance was extended to India. A few weeks earlier the American Government had given Japan a free hand in Korea in return for a pledge respecting the Philippines (Taft-Katsura Memorandum). On December 21, 1905, Japan established a protectorate in Korea. Meanwhile, the French, worried about Indochina and the possibility of becoming involved in a war with England, signed a treaty with the Japanese in June, 1907, in which each recognized the other's special interests in the Far East. In the summer of 1907 the Russians and Japanese came together and signed a number of agreements, among them a secret protocol dividing Manchuria. In the meantime American-Japanese relations had been deteriorating as a result of anti-Japanese measures on the Pacific coast and of the closed door policy Japan was pursuing in Manchuria. In 1907 there was serious fear of war. President Theodore Roosevelt met this situation by using a combination of the big stick—the world cruise of the U.S. fleet—and the soft answer—the American-Japanese Arbitration Convention (May, 1908), the "gentlemen's agreement" (February, 1907). The Japanese were under the impression that they had obtained American recognition of their special position in Manchuria by the Root-Takahira Notes (November, 1908), but they were soon disabused when Secretary of State Knox proposed in December, 1909, the internationalization of Manchuria's railroads. Russia and Japan responded by signing a treaty (July, 1910), which pledged them to common action in the defence of their interests. A month later Japan annexed Korea. In 1912 the Russo-Japanese alliance was further strengthened by a treaty reaffirming the division of Manchuria and giving the western half of Inner Mongolia to Russia, the eastern half to Japan.

Domestic Politics 1905-14. The Japanese public was furious when it learned that the Portsmouth Treaty contained no indemnity. Rioting broke out in Tokyo. Martial law was declared and Katsura resigned. Saionji Kimmochi, a protégé of Ito and his successor as president of the *Seiyukai,* became Prime Minister. During his ministry the trunk railroads were nationalized. He finally resigned in July, 1908, because he was unsuccessful in persuading the military to cut their estimates. Katsura, supported by Saionji's *Seiyukai,* returned to power. In August, 1911, he resigned because of budgetary difficulties, and was again replaced by Saionji. Saionji, having decided that the nation was spending beyond its means, adopted a retrenchment policy and sought to postpone the naval expansion program and the creation of two new army divisions. The Army Minister, General Uehara, opposed this economy move and, when Saionji persisted, resigned in December, 1912. Since the Army would not provide another minister, Saionji had to leave office, despite the fact his *Seiyukai* had won an overwhelming victory at the polls in May. At this point Katsura, who had left active politics to become an Imperial Household official, returned to the scene. He secured an imperial order commanding the Navy, which had refused to recommend a minister, to supply him with one and proceeded to organize a cabinet. The outraged *Seiyukai* rose in opposition. Katsura organized his own party in the Diet but was not able to obtain a majority. He then arranged for Saionji to receive an imperial command ordering him to have the *Seiyukai* support the Cabinet. Rather than do this Saionji resigned the party presidency. Katsura's misuse of the Emperor's prestige so aroused public feeling that on February 10, 1913, tens of thousands rioted throughout Tokyo. On February 11, Katsura yielded office and from that time on the imperial rescript could no longer be used as a political weapon. Admiral Yamamoto Gombei, the new Prime Minister, loosened the requirements for service ministers by making eligible inactive as well as active officers, but this had no practical effect. Yamamoto himself was forced to resign in April, 1914, because of revelations of corruption in the Navy (Siemens Affair). The *genro* then turned to the old warhorse, Okuma. The Army made some difficulty, but agreed to supply a minister when Okuma promised to give them the two new divisions.

Economic Developments 1894-1913. During this period the Japanese banking system took shape. In 1882 the Bank of Japan had been established as the central bank and two years before that the Yokohama Specie Bank had been set up to handle the financing of foreign trade. In 1896 the Hypothec Bank was organized to provide long-term credits secured by real property. Four years later the Industrial Bank of Japan was created to make long-term loans on the security of negotiable instruments. As Japan expanded overseas, financial institutions were devised to aid in the economic exploitation of the new territories: in 1899, the Bank of Formosa (Taiwan); in 1908, the Oriental Development Company; and in 1909, the Bank of Korea. It was through these semi-official banks that the Government directed credit into areas of the economy which it desired to see developed.

State finance saw great changes in this period. There was a phenomenal growth in the size of the budget. Before the Sino-Japanese War the budget had amounted to only about 80,000,000 yen, but by 1913 it was up to 600,000,000 yen. This vast expansion was largely accounted for by increases in expenditures for military purposes, for the development of industries which might not be profitable but which were considered important to national defense, and for investment in the overseas empire. The increases in outgo were provided for in two ways. First, the Government increased its revenues by introducing a sharp rise in tax rates and by instituting monopolies in tobacco and camphor. Second, a number of foreign loans were floated, so that by 1913 well over 80 per cent of Japan's national debt was held by foreigners. In view of its successes in the Sino-Japanese and Russo-Japanese War the Government now felt it could safely reverse its former policy of avoiding foreign loans. These same successes had made Japan an acceptable field of investment to foreigners. The result was that local governments and private firms were also able to make loans. Japan, which in 1893 had been neither a debtor nor a creditor nation, had by 1913 become a debtor nation to the amount of more than a billion two hundred million yen.

In 1913 Japan had a population of about 51,000,000. Since the early 1870's there had been an increase of 47 per cent. Until 1900 most of this increase was absorbed by the countryside, but after that date it was reflected in the growth of urban centers. By 1913 only 72 per cent of the population were living in places under 10,000. More than half were still engaged in agriculture. Rice production went up by 30 per cent, but after 1900 Japan had to begin importing food. A plentiful supply of labor combined with a small amount of arable land—only 16 per cent of the land area—made the typical farm a small one. In 1910 two-thirds of the farms were under 2½ acres. Moreover, since the Restoration there had been a sharp increase in the amount of tenancy. Between 1868 and 1910 the percentage of arable land under tenancy rose from 20 to 45 per cent. Only about one-fourth of

the farmers owned all the land they worked. Tenants
paid 45 to 60 per cent of their crop in rent.

During these two decades Japanese industry made
tremendous strides. By 1914 there were almost a million
persons working in factories. The greatest development
came in the field of textiles since Japan's traditions, the
abundance of cheap female labor, and the relative inex-
pensiveness of textile machinery gave her an advantage
here. Three-fifths of the factory workers were engaged
in this segment of the economy. The heavy industries and
machine tools also made progress at this time. In 1901
the Government iron works at Yawata came into operation and a number of private firms were founded, but
in 1913 these sources supplied only 48 per cent of the
pig iron and 23 per cent of the steel required by the
nation. Japan was handicapped in this field by a lack of
iron ore and coking coal. The large investment required
in heavy industry and machine tools resulted in the
domination of these fields by the *Zaibatsu,* whose private
banks were a convenient source of funds. Under a policy
of government subsidies, the merchant marine expanded
steadily. By 1913 it amounted to one and a half million
tons and carried half of the foreign trade. The heavily
subsidized shipbuilding industry also made progress, and
by World War I it was able to construct warships.

During these years the foreign trade of Japan increased
about seven times and by the end of the period averaged
more than a billion yen a year. Raw silk, silk goods,
cotton yarn, and cotton goods constituted over half of
the exports. In 1913 Japan supplied one-fourth of the
world cotton yarn exports. This amazing rise in exports
was made possible by the general world prosperity and
the absence of trade barriers. While Japan's trade balance
had been usually favorable from 1881 to 1893, this
period was characterized by a heavy deficit both in invisible and visible items. Japan balanced her international accounts with the proceeds of the foreign loans mentioned
previously. However, by the end of 1913 she was in
desperate straits and it seemed that her finances would
collapse if there were no halt in the expansion of her
military and colonial development expenses.

World War I. Despite the opposition of a large

segment of English public opinion, the Anglo-Japanese Alliance had been extended in 1911 for another ten years. The British Government felt this was necessary in order to free naval vessels for duty in the Atlantic. When war broke out in August, 1914, the British asked the Japanese to destroy German naval vessels in the Far East, but they refrained from asking for a declaration of war for fear of what Japan might do in China and the Pacific islands. The Okuma Cabinet decided to enter the war despite a specific British request to the contrary. On August 15, 1914, the Japanese sent Germany an ultimatum demanding that she withdraw all warships from Chinese and Japanese waters, or disarm them, and that Kiaochow leasehold (Shantung) be surrendered to Japan "with a view to eventual restoration of the same to China." When the Germans made no reply, Japan declared war on August 23, 1914. Tsingtao fell on November 7, and the Japanese took over the leasehold territory and all German interests in Shantung province. Japanese troops also began, despite Chinese protests, to police all the province's railroads. Meanwhile, the Japanese Navy occupied the German Pacific islands. After that, ignoring Allied requests that troops and ships be sent to Europe, Japan limited her participation in the war to convoy duty in the Indian Ocean and Mediterranean.

Economic Effects of World War I. On the eve of World War I, Japan's economy was in a serious state financially. By the end of 1913 the international accounts situation had become so tight that the Government was contemplating raising a foreign loan in order to pay the interest on the already existing foreign debt. The outbreak of World War I came as a godsend for Japan. Orders poured in from the Allied Powers with price no object. Neutral markets the world over, but especially in Asia, turned to the Japanese for the goods that the Western industrial nations could no longer supply. Exports increased by 40 per cent in bulk and by 300 per cent in value. There was a tremendous expansion in the range and volume of industrial production. The number of workers in factories rose 70 per cent. The merchant marine doubled in size and increased its earnings ten times over. The favorable balance of visible and invisible trade enjoyed by Japan from 1914 to 1919 gave her a net gain in her international accounts of more than three billion yen. Japan suddenly changed from a debtor nation to a creditor nation, and the rest of the world owed her more than a billion yen.

The Twenty-one Demands. For the first few years after the Sino-Japanese War Japan's policy toward China was to prevent China from being parceled out among the Powers, for she did not yet feel strong enough to compete in such a division. The Japanese Government was, therefore, friendly to groups such as the reformers of 1898 and Sun Yat-sen, since it felt that only modernization could save China. This attitude changed after the Russo-Japanese War. By the Komura Treaty of 1905 the Chinese Government recognized the transfer to Japan of Russia's rights in southern Manchuria. This and other actions convinced Japan she could rely on the cooperation of the Manchu dynasty. In 1907 the Japanese Government even felt obliged to ask Sun to leave Japan, although they softened the blow with a gift of 70,000 yen. A primary concern of Japan was the coal mines, iron mines and iron works held in central China by the Hanyehp'ing Company, an enterprise which was felt to be vitally important to operation of the Yawata Iron Works. In the 1900's a number of Japanese loans had been made to this company in an effort to secure control of its output.

The Chinese Revolution of 1911 caught the Japanese Government unawares and without a policy. They were unable to decide which faction to support and did not, therefore, have a great influence on the struggle for power. Yuan Shih-k'ai emerged victorious, but Sun Yat-sen was also part of the Government. In 1913 Sun came to Japan and in cooperation with prominent Japanese businessmen set up the Chinese Industrial Corporation, a *Zaibatsu* financial operation. But in China Yuan suddenly crushed Sun's party and assumed dictatorial powers. Both the Japanese and Yuan began to contend for control of the Hanyehp'ing Company. Yuan resolved the issue in China's favor by issuing in November, 1914, a presidential decree nationalizing the mines. This was followed in January, 1915, by an order abolishing the Shantung war zone.

For several months a growing opinion in Japan held that, with the Western Powers busy fighting one another, there was now a golden opportunity to settle the China question in a manner favorable to Japan. Japan's capital shortage put her at a disadvantage in competing with the Western nations for economic rights in China. Now seemed a ripe time to obtain those rights by political pressure and in the process secure Japan's interests in Manchuria, in Shantung, and in the Hanyehp'ing Company. The Japanese ambassador, acting under the instructions of Okuma's Foreign Minister, Kato Komei, on January 18, 1915, gave President Yuan a secret note embodying 21 demands. (*See Reading No. 8.*) These demands were divided into five groups. Group One would have given Japan Germany's rights in Shantung plus additional railroad building privileges. Group Two extended the term of Japan's rights in Manchuria from the original 25 years to 99 years and enlarged the Japanese scope of activity there. Group Three gave Japan control of the Hanyehp'ing Company and its production. Group Four prohibited China from ceding or leasing "to a third power any harbor or bay or island along the coast of China." Group Five provided that the Chinese were to employ Japanese political, financial, and military advisers, that Japan share in policing important cities, that additional railroad concessions be given, and that Japan be granted a monopoly on mine, harbor, and railroad development in Fukien.

When the Chinese leaked these demands to the public, such was the reaction within China and in the larger world that the Japanese had to modify their position. The final agreements, signed May 25, 1915, made Shantung a Japanese sphere of influence in return for the retrocession of the leasehold; extended Japan's Manchurian rights to 99 years; and gave her exclusive rights to build railroads and harbors in Fukien. Japan had to remain content with this until death removed Yuan and China collapsed into the warlord era. Then Japan was able, by advancing the Nishihara loans to the corrupt

Anfu clique in Peking, to secure special military privileges which remained in force until the fall of the clique in 1920. The Anfu clique also secretly agreed to recognize Japan's position in Shantung.

The 1918 Rice Riots. In October, 1916, Okuma resigned the prime ministership and recommended that Kato Komei, who was then organizing a new political party—the *Kenseikai* (Constitutional Association)—be given the position. The *genro,* now only Matsukata, Yamagata, and Saionji, were opposed to Kato, who had made no secret of his hostility to Yamagata and, while Foreign Minister, had discontinued sending them copies of the ministry's materials. They rejected Okuma's suggestion for the prime ministership and chose General Count Terauchi, the Governor-General of Korea. Terauchi dissolved the hostile Diet, and in the ensuing elections the *Seiyukai,* which supported the Government, gained a majority. One of the main problems confronting the Government was the level of prices, which had almost doubled since the outbreak of the war. Wages had risen too, but not as fast. As a result real wages had declined. In August, 1918, a number of Toyama fishing village women rioted against the high price of rice. When the movement spread throughout the country, troops had to be called in to end the tumult. Terauchi resigned in September, and this time the *genro's* choice fell on Hara Takashi, the man to whom Saionji had yielded the *Seiyukai* presidency in 1913. Hara was the first prime minister without a title of nobility and the first one to emerge from the lower house of the Diet. Hara's program might be summed up as expansion of education, of communications, of industry, and of armaments. He remained on good terms with the *genro* and the House of Peers. Since he himself and several of his ministers were former bureaucrats, his relations with the bureaucracy were smooth. His well-disciplined majority in the lower house relieved him of any worries in this area. He did little, however, to advance parliamentary government. He made his decisions in consultation with extra-party powers and then told the party what it was expected to do. His cabinet was still functioning smoothly when a simpleton's dagger struck him down on November 4, 1921. His Finance Minister,

Takahashi Korekiyo, became Prime Minister, but he was unable to hold the party factions together and resigned in June, 1922.

The Siberian Expedition. In July, 1918, the Western Allies decided to send troops into Siberia. The decision was motivated not only by a desire to rescue the Czech troops marooned there and to establish an eastern front, but also by the fear that Japan would act alone. Already, in April, 1918, a Japanese naval landing party had briefly occupied Vladivostok. To the Japanese military leaders the chaotic conditions in Russia seemed to offer an unequaled opportunity to take over eastern Siberia or at least to set up a friendly buffer state there. There was much opposition in Japanese Government circles to this kind of thinking, even Terauchi being unsure of the wisdom of the step. But the Army was insistent. When the Allied expedition landed, Japan sent in some 75,000 troops—three times the combined number of other Allied troops. After the Western troops withdrew in 1920, the Japanese Army remained. In that same year they used the murder of some Japanese at the Siberian town of Nicolaievsk as an excuse to occupy Russian Sakhalin. By this time the huge expense of the operation and lack of results had made the venture extremely unpopular, but when the Washington Conference met the Japanese troops were still in Siberia.

The Japanese at Versailles. While World War I was still in progress Japan endeavored to safeguard her gains in China by reaching understandings with the other Powers. In July, 1916, Russia and Japan entered into a five-year defensive alliance designed to protect their China interests. Early in 1917 secret treaties with Russia, England, Italy, and France recognized Japanese claims to Shantung and the German Pacific islands north of the equator. American approval also seemed to be given in the Lansing-Ishii Notes (November 2, 1917). Although the Japanese delegation at Versailles was primarily interested in Shantung and the Pacific islands, it was also anxious to secure some statement of racial equality. Consequently, it proposed that a race equality clause be included in the Covenant of the League of Nations. However, Australian opposition and Wilson's fear of the

Pacific coast's reaction resulted in its rejection. The Pacific islands were mandated to Japan as a matter of course, but the opposition of the Chinese delegates created a great stir over the transfer of Germany's Shantung rights. In the end Japan received what she wanted, for Wilson, the only important delegate who opposed the transfer, yielded in order to prevent the Japanese from walking out as the Italians had done. In the arrangements for the League of Nations, Japan was made one of the five permanent members of the council and was thus formally recognized as a world power.

The Washington Conference. By 1920 Japan, England, and the United States were in a full-scale naval race, as a result of which there was widespread talk of a coming war between America and Japan. This was particularly disturbing to countries like Australia and Canada, which had no desire to become embroiled in a war with the United States through the operation of the Anglo-Japanese Alliance. There was also a widespread revolt among taxpayers against the burden of armaments. Because of these pressures, the leading naval powers were finally induced to hold a naval limitations conference at Washington beginning in November, 1921. Since unrest in the Pacific was a prime source for fear of war, the naval conference became, in effect, a Far Eastern conference. Three important treaties came out of this conference. First, on December 13, 1921, France, England, Japan, and the United States signed the Four-Power Pact providing for the maintenance of the *status quo* in the Pacific. This treaty also terminated the Anglo-Japanese Alliance. On February 6, 1922, the Five Power Naval Treaty was concluded. It provided for the scrapping of several hundred thousand tons of capital ships; established a 5:5:3 ratio for the United States, England, and Japan; established a 35,000 limit for capital ships and 27,000 tons for aircraft carriers; declared a 10-year naval holiday; and set over-all tonnage limits for capital ships. In addition, it provided that the *status quo* be maintained on fortifications between, roughly, Hawaii and Singapore. This pact was advantageous to Japan, for it meant that her fleet could not be challenged in East Asiatic waters by either England or the United States acting alone. It also saved her from the financial ruin of a naval race.

The third treaty was the Nine-Power Pact, signed February 6, 1922, designed "to respect and observe the territorial integrity and political and administrative independence of the Chinese Republic." While the Conference was in session, the Japanese and Chinese carried on conversations about the Shantung question. Japan agreed to restore the leasehold and withdraw her troops in six months. The Tsingtao-Tsinan railway was returned to China, but China was to pay Japan its assessed value, Japan participating in its management until payment was completed. Japan also announced at the Washington Conference that she would withdraw from Siberia as soon as it was possible. In October, 1922, the last Japanese troops left the Maritime Province, but northern Sakhalin continued to be occupied.

— 3 —

FROM THE WASHINGTON CONFERENCE TO V-J DAY

Return to Non-party Cabinets. When Takahashi's *Seiyukai* cabinet fell in June, 1922, the *genro* did not offer the prime ministership to Kato Komei, the leader of the opposition *Kenseikai,* but turned instead to Admiral Kato Tomosaburo, Takahashi's Navy Minister. The *Seiyukai* immediately pledged him its support in order to avoid a *Kenseikai* cabinet. Admiral Kato was undoubtedly chosen because the *genro* felt that only a well-established military leader would be able to carry through the naval disarmament program and withdraw the Army from Siberia. Admiral Kato, whose cabinet did not include any party men, died in August, 1923. Again the *genro* chose a non-party Prime Minister, Admiral Yamamoto Gombei, who returned to organize his second cabinet. Yamamoto invited into his cabinet the three most important party leaders—Takahashi (*Seiyukai*), Kato (*Kenseikai*), and Inukai Tsuyoshi (*Kakushin* Club). However, only Inukai accepted, and for this he was roundly denounced as a betrayer of the party movement. The Cabinet only lasted through December, 1923, when it resigned because an attempt had been made on the life of Crown Prince Hirohito.

Once again the *genro*, Matsukata and Saionji, rejected a party cabinet, this time recommending Count Kiyoura Keigo, a former bureaucrat who was now in the House of Peers. Kiyoura formed his cabinet largely out of fellow ex-bureaucrats from the House of Peers. The three party leaders—Takahashi, Kato, and Inukai—immediately decided to organize a coalition movement to force a return to party cabinets. In this they were joined by the Tokyo newspapermen. But over half of the *Seiyukai* Diet members seceded and, under Tokonami Takejiro, formed a new party, the *Seiyu Honto*, which supported Kiyoura. Since the Cabinet still did not have a majority, it dissolved the Diet. The election held in May, 1924, was an overwhelming victory for the coalition. Kiyoura resigned and the sole surviving *genro*, Saionji, impressed by the public's solid support for Kato Komei, asked him to become Prime Minister. On June 11, 1924, Kato organized a three-party coalition cabinet.

Social Stirrings. The propaganda for democracy incident to the ideological side of World War I could not help but have some effect in Japan. To this in 1917 was added the impact of the Russian Revolution. As a result there developed a popular movement for universal suffrage and for the establishment of a true parliamentary democracy. The leaders in this movement were such professors as Yoshino Sakuzo, of Tokyo Imperial University. Under the influence of these men, students soon began to organize themselves into clubs and societies for the discussion of political and social problems. In 1918 Yoshino organized the *Reimeikai*, a group dedicated to popularizing democratic ideas. By 1924 the student groups were united in a National Federation of Societies for the Study of Social Science. The press also developed a liberal tone, and such magazines as *Chuo Koron* and such newspapers as the *Tokyo Asahi* became vehicles for the spread of new ideas. The atmosphere created by these activities was largely responsible for the success of the parties in 1924.

Toward the end of the war, labor began to bestir itself and the union movement became prominent. There had been attempts in the 1890's to organize trade unions, but they had been unsuccessful. The Peace Preservation Act of 1900 placed such restrictions on labor groups that it was impossible for them to operate. In 1912, however, Suzuki Bunji established the *Yuaikai,* a kind of labor benevolent society based on the principle of labor-capital cooperation. The economic difficulties of 1918-19 resulted in the formation of a number of unions, and in 1921 Suzuki transformed his *Yuaikai* into the Japan Federation of Labor Unions. By 1927 there were more than five hundred associations with a membership of over 300,000. However, the members represented only about 15 per cent of Japan's factory labor, which was difficult to organize because it consisted, to a large extent, of temporary girl workers. The new militant attitude of labor was typified by the Kawasaki Shipyard strike in July, 1921, when 30,000 workers demonstrated in the Kobe streets.

Until the 1920's the Government had demonstrated little interest in protecting labor. A Mining Act was passed in 1905 and a Factory Act in 1911, but the enforcement of both was delayed until 1916 in order to allow employers to adjust themselves. These acts, applying only to units employing fifteen or more workers, established an eleven-hour day for women and children under 15 as well as a minimum employment age of 12. In 1921 a Social Bureau was set up in the Home Ministry to look after labor's affairs. The following year a Health Insurance Act was passed. Then in 1923 the Factory Act was amended. The working day for women and children was reduced to ten hours and the minimum working age raised to fourteen. The law was not applied until 1926 and, for most of the textile industries, not until 1931. In 1929 work after 11 P.M. was abolished for women and children. The only regulation of male hours occurred in 1930-32, when a ten-hour maximum was established for mining, construction, communication, and transport workers.

The Left Wing Political Movement. An Oriental Socialist Party, actually a local agrarian group, was organized as early as 1882, but it was immediately dissolved by the Government. The real origin of the left-wing movement occurred in 1898, when a small group organized an Association for the Study of Socialism. This was expanded in 1901 into a Social Democratic Party, which was suppressed by the Government on the very day it was founded. There were several other unsuccessful attempts to establish a party, but then the movement was split by a quarrel between those advocating parliamentary action and those advocating violence. In the summer of 1910 the Government, which had been bending every effort to destroy the movement, arrested Kotoku Denjiro and several others for plotting to kill the Emperor Meiji. After a quick, secret trial Kotoku and eleven others were executed. Public shock at the enormity of the crime charged against Kotoku resulted in the disappearance of the Socialist movement.

The ferment of thought during the war led to a revival of Socialist thought. In 1920 the Japan Socialists' Union came into existence but was immediately suppressed. However, various intellectuals, labor union leaders, and farm leaders continued their endeavors to organize politically. These efforts were intensified after universal manhood suffrage was adopted in 1925. In December of that year a Farmer-Labor Party was established, but it was dissolved by the Government within three hours on the grounds it was Communist-dominated. Other parties were organized in the 1920's, but when they were not being harassed by the Government, they were splintering into fragments because of ideological differences. Proletariat parties did manage to win eight seats in the 1928 election and five in 1930. By 1932 the moderate and conservative Socialists had united in the Social Mass Party and were subsequently able to make substantial gains at the polls.

The Kenseikai Cabinets. The Kato coalition cabinet was responsible for the passage of several important measures. In March, 1925, the Manhood Suffrage Bill was enacted. This permitted every Japanese male over the age of 25 to vote, so that the electorate was expanded from three million voters to well over twelve million. But in order to prevent extension of the suffrage leading to radical agitation, the same Diet passed a Peace Preservation Act which made it illegal to advocate the alteration of Japan's political structure or the abolition of private property, under penalty of imprisonment up to ten years. Another policy of the Cabinet was military retrenchment. It managed, with the cooperation of War Minister Ugaki, to cut the Army by four divisions, but this was only done at a price. A system of military training was set up in the universities and secondary schools, and the money saved by the reduction in strength was used to modernize the Army's equipment.

Kato's Foreign Minister, Shidehara Kijuro, adopting a conciliatory attitude toward China, tried to undo the damage of Shantung and the Twenty-one Demands. Shidehara had no intention of yielding any of Japan's rights in southern Manchuria. In China proper, nevertheless, he felt Japan must learn to adjust herself to Chinese nationalism and, by aiding rather than retarding China's development, build a friendship that would be useful in allowing a peaceful expansion of Japan's economic activities. As a consequence, he avoided the use of force in China and always endeavored to settle incidents by negotiation. Shidehara also established normal relations with Russia. The Russo-Japanese Treaty of 1925 provided for the Soviet acceptance of the Portsmouth Treaty, the granting of fishing rights, and the adjustment of the Tsarist debts. Japan agreed to withdraw from northern Sakhalin and received in return oil, coal, and timber concessions. Both countries promised not to engage in propaganda activities endangering each other's security or domestic order.

Kato and his *Kenseikai* were very anxious to reduce government expenditures and balance the budget. In this they ran afoul of the *Seiyukai,* and in August, 1925, the Cabinet was reorganized, becoming a purely *Kenseikai* body. A few months later, Kato suddenly died and his place as Prime Minister and party head was assumed by Wakatsuki Reijiro, the Home Minister. The *Kenseikai,* which had only a plurality in the Diet, managed to con-

trol the lower house by entering into a working alliance
with the *Seiyu Honto*. In the spring of 1927 there occurred
a serious economic crisis, which the Cabinet attempted to
meet by means of an emergency financial decree authorizing the Bank of Japan to lend 200,000,000 yen. The
Privy Council refused its assent to this measure, whereupon Wakatsuki decided to resign. The president of the
Seiyukai, General Baron Tanaka Giichi, who had retired
from the Army to become a politician, was then asked
to undertake the formation of a new cabinet.

The Economic Crisis of 1927.   In March, 1920, the
economic boom that the war had created and postwar
reconstruction sustained finally came to an end. When
prices began to fall precipitously, the Government intervened and, by authorizing the Bank of Japan to make
substantial loans, halted the downward trend. It did this
because the assets of the commercial banking system
were tied up in loans to various companies; if the value
of the materials held by these companies fell too far, the
solvency of the banking system would be threatened. The
Government hoped that, given time, these debts could
be gradually adjusted and a crisis avoided. As a result
of this policy, Japanese prices were maintained at a level
above that of the rest of the world. Consequently Japanese exports declined while imports went up, and Japan
began to experience great difficulties balancing her foreign accounts. To complicate matters, the Great Earth-
quake of 1923 necessitated an extension of additional
credits with a corresponding rise in prices. The retrenchment program of the Kato and Wakatsuki cabinets was
aimed at bringing down prices, so that exports could be
expanded and the foreign trade brought into balance. In
the spring of 1927, a Diet discussion of the Government's
financial plans resulted in the general public discovering
that the Bank of Formosa had a substantial portion of its
funds tied up in worthless loans. A run developed on
this bank and soon spread to many others. It was to stop
this run that the Wakatsuki cabinet had wanted the
emergency financial decree mentioned above. Since the
Privy Council had prevented the Government from giving
help, the Bank of Formosa and thirty-five other banks
had to close their doors. The Tanaka cabinet declared a

moratorium and then issued, with the Privy Council's approval, an emergency financial decree authorizing the Bank of Japan to lend 700,000,000 yen to the banks.

This financial crisis had several important results. First, it eliminated many unsound companies and improved the competitive position of Japanese industry. Second, it resulted in an increased control of the Japanese economy by the *Zaibatsu*. Since their banks had not been involved in the crisis, an increasing percentage of deposits flowed to them and thus strengthened their capital resources. The *Zaibatsu* also took advantage of company failures to buy up plants and round out their industrial empires.

The Tanaka Cabinet. Despite the fact that Tanaka had come to the *Seiyukai* from the Army, he organized a cabinet which consisted, aside from the service ministers, completely of party members. This was more than could be said for most other "party" cabinets. The new Cabinet completely reversed the financial policies of its predecessor and embarked upon a program of large budgets and deficit spending. Perhaps the most noteworthy aspect of Tanaka's internal policy was his zealous attempt to root out radical thought, especially communism.

The Japanese Communist Party was founded in Tokyo on July 5, 1922. As soon as the police learned of its existence there were mass round-ups. As a result of the attempted assassination of Hirohito December, 1923, police action was intensified, and by 1924 all but a few of the party were in jail. A few new leaders smuggled in from Russia carefully built the party up again, and by 1927 it had reached a substantial size. On March 15, 1928, the Tanaka Cabinet staged nationwide raids which netted about 1,500 Communist suspects. A year later, in April, 1929, another 1,000 suspects were arrested. Other cabinets continued the hunt; by 1935 there was no more organized Communist activity in Japan. In connection with this anti-radical drive the Tanaka Cabinet issued an emergency decree increasing the penalty for violating certain sections of the 1925 Peace Preservation Law from the old maximum of ten years' imprisonment to death. In April, 1928, the Cabinet also banned student associations for the study of "social science." The eagerness of the Tanaka Cabinet to suppress radical activities was matched by the other party cabinets. Under none of them was there any relaxation of the police's strict censorship of all the publication media.

Tanaka, who was his own foreign minister, decided to adopt a stronger policy toward China than Shidehara had followed. (*See Reading No. 9.*) Shortly after the Cabinet took office, troops were dispatched to Shantung on the plea that the disturbances created by the Kuomintang move into the north were endangering Japanese lives and property. These troops were withdrawn when Chiang K'ai-shek decided to suspend operations. As soon as Chiang again moved northward, the Japanese rushed troops to the city of Tsinan (in Shantung). There in May, 1928, fighting broke out between the Japanese and the Kuomintang troops. The Japanese seized control of the city and were gradually withdrawn from the province only after the Chinese agreed to make an apology and pay an indemnity. The incident resulted in a flare-up of anti-Japanese feeling. Meanwhile, at about the same time a group of Japanese Army officers, by assassinating the warlord of Manchuria, Chang Tso-lin, had endeavored to create an excuse for taking over Manchuria. This incident had two effects. It resulted in the rapprochement between Chang's heir, Chang Hsueh-liang, and the Kuomintang, thus endangering Japan's position in Manchuria. It also eventually resulted in Tanaka being forced to resign his post in July, 1929.

The Hamaguchi-Wakatsuki Cabinets. After the fall of the Wakatsuki Cabinet in 1927, the *Kenseikai* and *Seiyu Honto* merged to form the *Minseito*. The president of this party, Hamaguchi Yuko, now became Prime Minister. Shidehara returned as Foreign Minister and, once again, Japan adopted a conciliatory policy toward China. By 1929 Japan had not yet closed the gap between her import and her exports. The Hamaguchi Cabinet undertook a program of retrenchment in government finance in order to bring about a price fall which would increase Japan's ability to compete on the world markets. It also launched a vigorous campaign to encourage decreased private consumption and increased use of home products. To help industry cut costs and reduce export prices, it organized a "rationalization movement."

Because budget reduction would be difficult without armament cuts, the Hamaguchi Cabinet entered with a will into the London Naval Conference of 1930. The naval treaty which was finally agreed on extended the Washington Conference ratio to cruisers and other smaller categories of vessels. The Japanese Navy was reluctant to accept this decision, and open dissension broke out in Tokyo. Hamaguchi finally got the Navy's consent, but only at the cost of an agreement giving the Chief of the Navy General Staff a veto over future agreements. In addition, most of the money saved under the treaty had to be given the Navy to expand its air force and other units not limited by the treaty. So much anti-Government feeling was aroused in ultranationalist circles that, on November 14, 1930, Hamaguchi was shot by a young fanatic. Another reason for Hamaguchi's unpopularity lay in his economic program. Just as it was put into operation, the 1929 world depression struck. From 1929 to 1930 Japanese exports dropped more than 30 per cent in value. Both agriculture and industry were reduced to an extremely unfavorable condition. The *Minseito* Cabinet, which was assigned a large share of the blame for these sufferings, came increasingly under attack. Hamaguchi survived until August, 1931, but he resigned as Prime Minister in April. Wakatsuki Reijiro succeeded him, keeping much the same cabinet and the same policies.

The Growth of Ultranationalism. In the 1920's the proponents of ultranationalist thought were just as numerous and active as the liberals. As early as 1918, Okawa Shumei had established the *Rosokai* to combat the influence of Yoshino Sakuzo. In 1919 the *Dai Nihon Kokusuikai* (Greater Japan National Essence Society) was set up under very prominent auspices and eventually came to have a million members. In 1924 Baron Hiranuma Kiichiro founded the *Kokuhonsha* (National Foundation Society), an organization dedicated to protecting Japan's national polity. Hiranuma was an ex-bureaucrat who was to become vice-president and then president of the Privy Council as well as Prime Minister. There were few prominent politicians, admirals, generals, or businessmen who were not members of this organization. In this period the Young Men's and Young Women's Associations, which reached into every village in the land, became channels for dispensing patriotic thought. This same function had long been performed by the Imperial Reservists Association. As the depression of the late 1920's and early 1930's bit deeper into the countryside, as the rice price fell and the raw silk market vanished, hundreds of little ultranationalist groups began to appear in the villages. There was wide variety among them, but they had certain features in common—they were against party government and they were against capitalism. And they were ready to use violence.

Since most of the Army conscripts came from the villages, unrest soon communicated itself to the Army. In the late 1920's most of the younger Army officers came from middle-class families in the villages or small rural towns and were sympathetic to the complaints arising from these quarters. Among these young officers small societies came into existence. A prime example is the *Sakurakai* (the Cherry Society) organized among field-grade officers in Tokyo in September, 1930. By March, 1931, the Sakurakai concocted a plot to establish a military dictatorship and only failed to put it into operation because the senior generals refused to play their allotted roles. Another group of officers and civilians plotted to assassinate the whole cabinet and seize control of the Government. By the sheerest accident the plot was discovered and the leaders arrested on October 16, 1931, eight days before the scheduled date of execution.

The Manchurian Incident. By the summer of 1931 Sino-Japanese tension over Manchuria had reached the exploding point. The warlord, Chang Hsueh-liang, was drawing closer and closer to the Nanking Government and permitting the Kuomintang to flood Manchuria with "rights recovery" propaganda. The Chinese were making it a policy to use native capital for the region's economic development. Gradually, a network of Chinese railroads was being built to parallel the Japanese South Manchurian Railroad system and direct the flow of goods to Chinese-controlled ports like Yingkow and Hulutao rather than Japanese Dairen. By June, 1931, Japanese negotiations to solve this railroad problem had ended in failure. It seemed as if the carefully constructed Japanese position in Manchuria was about to be lost. At this point the Japanese Army decided to settle the question by force. On September 18, 1932, without any prior consultation with the Wakatsuki Cabinet, an attack was launched. China immediately appealed to the League, which requested a cease-fire. But the Japanese Army had plans for developing Manchuria as an economic base and was not to be deterred by words. In December, the Lytton Commission was established by the League to investigate the issue on the spot. Shortly thereafter the Japanese Navy attacked the Chinese troops in Shanghai. This side war ended in May, 1932, but in the meantime an "independent" state, Manchukuo, had been created in Manchuria, and the last Manchu emperor, Henry Pu-yi, imported to become its titular ruler. In August the complete control of the Japanese Army was plainly indicated by the appointment of the commander of the Kwantung Army as both governor-general of the Kwantung Territory and ambassador to Manchukuo. In February, 1933, the League acted on the Lytton Report and adopted a non-recognition policy toward Manchukuo. On March 27, 1933, Japan announced that she was withdrawing from the League.

Disappearance of Party Cabinets. The second Wakatsuki Cabinet proved incapable of controlling the Army's activities in Manchuria. In December, 1931, it was finally forced out of office by its own Home Minister's refusal to attend Cabinet meetings. Adachi Kenzo, the Home Minister, had done this because he wished to bring a "national union" Cabinet to power. However, Saionji recommended the appointment of Inukai Tsuyoshi, who had become president of the *Seiyukai* in 1929 on the death of Tanaka. The new cabinet, enthusiastically backing the Army's venture in Manchuria, was willing to make large military appropriations. Social unrest was becoming dangerous. In February, 1932, Inoue Junnosuke, who as Finance Minister in the previous cabinet was popularly regarded as responsible to some extent for the economic depression, was killed by a member of an ultranationalist group. The following month Baron Dan Takuma, chairman of the Mitsui board of directors, was also assassinated. These crimes had been the work of a group of Navy officers, Army cadets, and civilians calling themselves the Blood Brotherhood. On May 15, 1932, this same group assassinated Prime Minister Inukai and assaulted the Tokyo central police headquarters, the Bank of Japan, the Mitsubishi Bank, the home of the chief official of the Imperial Household, and the *Seiyukai* headquarters. The attack was clearly aimed against the parties, the *Zaibatsu,* and the moderate advisers of the Emperor.

Since the Army refused to supply an Army Minister to another party cabinet, Saionji turned to a moderate military man, Admiral Saito Makoto, who in the past had shown himself to be sympathetic to responsible government. His cabinet included four *Seiyukai* and three *Minseito* ministers. The average Japanese was not too concerned when a party cabinet was not set up, for the parties had long since fallen into disrepute. In 1929-30 scandals involving Diet members had come to light and convinced the public that the parties were a mass of corrupt politicians interested only in money-making. Most Japanese felt that the parties were ultimately controlled by the *Zaibatsu*—the *Seiyukai* by the Mitsui, the *Minseito* by the Mitsubishi—and that the parties manipulated the Government in the interest of these financial groups. The new cabinet offered no serious opposition to the Army's Manchurian plans, but it was not able to satisfy extremist elements. The trial of the Blood Brotherhood dragged out and became a sounding board for ultranationalist and anticapitalist sentiment. A plot by a group calling itself the "God-sent Troops" was forestalled on the eve of its execution in July, 1933. This conspiracy called for the wholesale elimination of the Emperor's advisers and the Cabinet as well as the nation's party and business leaders.

Meanwhile, a systematic campaign was undertaken to eradicate liberal thought. Saito's Education Minister, Hatoyama Ichiro, dismissed Professor Takikawa of the Kyoto Imperial University Law School. The whole law faculty resigned in protest, but the Cabinet remained firm and discharged several other liberal professors. The pressure was maintained under the Cabinet of Admiral Okada, another Navy moderate, who succeeded Saito as

Prime Minister in July, 1934. By this time the great target of the "patriots" had become Professor Minobe Tatsukichi, for many years a distinguished professor of constitutional law at Tokyo Imperial University Law School. In his widely used textbooks on the Japanese Constitution, he had expressed the idea that the Emperor was an "organ," that is, an agency, of the State. Reactionary thinkers asserted this was an attack on the national polity and in 1935 organized a Federation for the Protection of the National Polity. Anti-Minobe resolutions were passed both in the House of Peers and the House of Representatives. The Army issued a notice to all its personnel denouncing the "organ theory." The Okada Cabinet finally issued an official statement rejecting the theory, and in September, 1935, Minobe resigned his seat in the House of Peers. This incident eventually resulted in the addition to the education ministry of a new bureau charged with spreading through the nation's school system a "clarification of national polity."

The February 1936 Incident. In the early 1930's there were a great number of shifting cliques within the Japanese Army. Broadly, however, there were two main lines of thought. One was represented by the *Kodo Ha* (Imperial Way Faction), a group of lower ranking officers who wished the Army to seize control and establish a species of state socialism. The other group, the *Tosei Ha* (Control Faction), consisted of higher Army officers who, while they favored extension of Army control at home and expansion abroad, wished to accomplish these aims within the existing social and economic framework. By 1934 the *Tosei Ha* was becoming disturbed by the violence of the *Kodo Ha* and decided to suppress its activities. As a first step, senior officers favoring the *Kodo Ha* were removed from positions of power. General Araki was forced out as War Minister in January, 1934, and General Mazaki as Inspector-General in July, 1935. General Nagata, the Army personnel chief, then began to transfer the *Kodo Ha* officers to posts remote from Tokyo. The growing rebellion of the *Kodo Ha* became evident in August, 1935, when a lieutenant-colonel, who had been transferred, walked into Nagata's office in the Army Ministry and killed him. The issue came to a head on February 26, 1936, when young officers of the First Division, which had received orders to go to Manchuria, mutinied and at the head of 1,400 troops seized central Tokyo. They attempted to assassinate Prime Minister Okada, who escaped and went into hiding. They succeeded, however, in killing the Army Inspector-General; the Finance Minister, Takahashi Korekiyo; and Admiral Saito, who had become Lord Privy Seal to the Emperor. It was not until February 29 that they were induced to surrender. Then the Army, determined to stamp out insubordination within its own ranks, quickly executed the leaders. The Army profited from this affair in two ways. First, the elimination of the anti-capitalist *Kodo Ha* made possible greater cooperation between the Army leaders and the *Zaibatsu*. Second, the civilian leaders in the Government became reluctant to oppose Army demands out of fear that another such uprising would occur.

The next Prime Minister was a professional diplomat, Hirota Koki. On March 9, 1936, he organized a cabinet whose composition was more or less dictated by the Army and gave assurances that he would be receptive to the Army's plans. In August, 1936, the Cabinet secretly decided upon a set of "Basic Principles for National Policy," which had largely been inspired by the Army. These principles called for continued overseas expansion; increased armaments in order to stabilize East Asia; the elimination of the U.S.S.R. as a threat to the cooperative economic development of Japan, China, and Manchukuo; and the extension of Japanese influence in Southeast Asia. Despite Hirota's compliance the Army wished to have one of its own generals named as Prime Minister. In January, 1937, the Army Minister resigned on the grounds that a Diet member had insulted him, but in reality to force Hirota out. Saionji attempted to have the moderate General Ugaki made Prime Minister, but the Army prevented this by refusing Ugaki an Army Minister. In the end the Army had its way and General Hayashi Senjuro was designated to form a cabinet. The Hayashi Cabinet was composed of military men and professional bureaucrats, indicating the strong ties which were developing between these two segments of the State. However,

Hayashi proved inept as an administrator. In June, 1937, he was replaced by Prince Konoe Fumimaro, a man who had managed to remain on friendly terms with all factions. Konoe had scarcely been in office a month, when the Sino-Japanese War began.

The Sino-Japanese War. In January, 1933, the Japanese Kwantung Army resumed military operations against China by seizing the Inner Mongolian province of Jehol, claiming that it was part of Manchukuo. It also sought to enter the North China province of Hopei, but here the Chinese troops put up a more successful resistance. Nevertheless, by the Tangku Truce (May 31, 1933), which ended the fighting, the Japanese made substantial gains. This agreement established a demilitarized zone extending from the Peiping-Tientsin area north to the Great Wall. All Chinese troops were to be withdrawn, and the responsibility for maintaining order was turned over to a police force friendly to Japan. It became quite clear that the Japanese Army was not content with Manchukuo but also intended to absorb North China. This impression was reinforced by the statement made in January, 1934, by Hirota Koki, then Foreign Minister, that Japan bore "the entire burden of responsibility" for the peace of East Asia. This was followed in April, 1934, by the famous Amau statement, which virtually proclaimed a Japanese "Monroe Doctrine" for East Asia and warned foreign nations against giving any kind of military, technological, or financial aid to China. (*See Reading No. 10.*)

In 1935 the Kwantung Army maintained military pressure along the Great Wall. By June they succeeded in getting the Chinese to agree to withdraw all their troops from Chahar, an Inner Mongolian province, and end all Kuomintang operations in the province. In July, the Ho-Umezu agreement made the same type of arrangement for Hopei province. Toward the end of the year the Japanese North China Army, stationed in the Peiping-Tientsin area under the Boxer Protocol, began to conspire with certain Chinese to establish a puppet government in the Hopei demilitarized zone. To forestall this action the Nanking Government was obliged to set up the autonomous Hopei-Chahar Political Council and, in effect, detach the area from central government control. In the meantime, Hirota, now become Prime Minister, had established, in October, 1935, a three-point program for the settlement of Sino-Japanese difficulties. China was to (1) repress anti-Japanese activity; (2) recognize Manchukuo; and (3) accept Japanese help in suppressing communism. Most of 1936 was spent in negotiations aimed at obtaining the Nanking Government's acceptance of these three points, but in November, 1936, a raid into Suiyuan province by Japanese-sponsored Mongolian troops caused the Chinese to break off the talks.

In the spring of 1937 the rising tide of anti-Japanese feeling among the Chinese people forced Chiang K'ai-shek to stiffen his attitude toward Japan and even to enter into truce negotiations with his inveterate foes, the Chinese communists. The General Staff in Tokyo was not anxious for war. A staff study made about this time recommended that the Army do nothing to arouse either the Chinese or the Russians. But the officers of the Japanese North China Army and the Kwantung Army had other ideas. As early as June, 1937, Tojo Hideki, then Chief of Staff of the Kwantung Army, warned Tokyo to strike before Chiang and the communists got together. Consequently, when on July 7, 1937, there was an incident at Lukouchiao (Marco Polo Bridge) involving Chinese and Japanese troops, the local Japanese officers permitted it to expand into a full-scale war despite the reluctance of the General Staff and the definite opposition of the Konoe Cabinet. By the end of July, North China had become a war area. In August, fighting broke out in Shanghai. The Japanese Government continued to negotiate with Nanking, but as Japanese successes multiplied the terms insisted on by the Army became greater and therefore less acceptable to the Chinese. City after city fell to the Japanese—Nanking (December, 1937), Canton (October, 1938), Hankow (October, 1938)—but as they advanced deeper into the interior, guerrilla warfare and the mountain escarpments brought them to a halt. Soon the China Incident became a stalemate, draining away Japanese human and material resources and offering little in return.

The New Order in Japan. The main work of the Konoe Cabinet, which took office on June 4, 1937, was to prepare the nation for the exigencies of the China war. Compulsory military training was instituted in all the schools and the conscription period was extended. At the insistence of the Army, which was worried about the physical condition of the nation's manpower, a Welfare Ministry was established and a National Health Insurance Law was put through the Diet. To give the Government policies proper backing a Cabinet Advisory Council was organized in October, 1937, and representatives of all factions appointed to it. At the same time, a Central Federation for National Spiritual Mobilization was created. The Education Ministry was turned over to General Araki, who fully utilized its potentialities for propagandizing. To coordinate the activities of the Government a Cabinet Planning Board had been established in May, 1937. In 1938, Konoe further streamlined Government decision-making by creating an inner cabinet consisting of himself, the Foreign Minister, the Finance Minister, the Army Minister and the Navy Minister. The most momentous step taken by the Cabinet was the passage in March, 1938 of the Mobilization Law, which gave the Government full power to dispose of all the resources of Japan and substituted government by decree for government by law.

Konoe resigned in January, 1939, to be followed in quick succession by three cabinets—the Hiranuma Cabinet (January-August, 1939), the General Abe Cabinet (August-January, 1940), and the Admiral Yonai Cabinet (January-July, 1940), all of which were noteworthy only for their inability to make decisions. On July 22, 1940, Konoe organized his second cabinet. Shortly thereafter he announced a sweeping program for "renovating" the nation. (*See Reading No. 11.*) While out of office he had been busy laying the foundation of a new party— the Imperial Rule Assistance Association. In July and August, all the political parties dissolved themselves and their members moved into the IRAA, which was formally inaugurated October 12, 1940. The new organization had a pyramidal structure reaching down into each rural village and city ward. Basically, it was a device for transmitting the Government's wishes to the people and for keeping in touch with public opinion.

The Japanese Economy in the 1930's. After the fall of the *Minseito* Cabinet in late 1931, the Japanese Government adopted an inflationary policy. This was largely the work of Takahashi Korekiyo, who was Finance Minister from December, 1931, to February, 1936. Takahashi was primarily interested in economic recovery, but the large increase in expenditure which occurred was mostly in the military portion of the budget. This rose from 31 per cent in 1931 to 47 per cent in 1936. Takahashi made no attempt to balance the budget by increasing taxes. Instead, he covered the annual deficit by selling bonds to the Bank of Japan and thereby increased the currency in circulation. This, in turn, resulted in the devaluation of the yen. By 1936 Takahashi, feeling that his purpose had been achieved, desired to return to a balanced budget. However, by this time the military had become so powerful in the Government that budgetary balancing was impossible, and Japan continued a policy of deficit financing up to and through World War II.

Takahashi's devaluation of the yen had an important effect on Japanese foreign trade—it cheapened Japanese goods in terms of foreign currencies and sparked an export boom. By 1936 the volume of Japan's exports had increased by 20 per cent over that of 1929. The mainstay of the export trade continued to be textiles, especially cotton, but a great variety of miscellaneous items was also becoming important. Although Japan greatly expanded her exports, it was largely at the cost of lowering her prices. Since the prices which she had to pay for imports increased, the terms upon which Japan was conducting her foreign trade became increasingly disadvantageous. Moreover, as competition for world markets became keener, an increasing number of restrictions developed in the form of tariffs and quota arrangements. This, of course, played into the hands of the Japanese expansionists who argued that their conquests were gaining Japan assured markets. But, paradoxically, the more Japan turned in that direction as a solution for her problems, the more she helped to destroy the very conditions essential to her economy—free trade and currency convertibility.

Between 1930 and 1940 the population of Japan rose from 64,450,000 to 73,114,000; by the latter year it was equally distributed among the rural and urban sections. Poor conditions continued in agriculture until the China war brought rising farm prices. In the 1930's there was a tremendous rise in the volume of Japanese industrial production, which from 1929 to 1939 increased by more than 80 per cent. Most of this increase was accounted for by the heavy industries, which multiplied their production over five times while light industrial production rose only about 20 per cent. By the end of the decade, light industries lost their predominance and heavy industries were responsible for almost three-quarters of the industrial output. All this reflected the growing concentration on armaments and on the production of capital goods for investment in both Japan proper and the overseas empire. This expansion of production was accompanied by a rise in technical efficiency and a broadening of the types of production. By 1937 Japan was able to produce almost all the machinery and machine tools needed by a modern industrial system. Until 1937 this remarkable growth was accomplished with almost no Governmental regulation, but afterwards growing competition among different segments of the economy for the factors of production forced the Government to adopt increasingly strict controls.

Japan's Relations with Germany and the U.S.S.R. Japan's seizure of Manchuria created an awkward position for the U.S.S.R., which controlled the Chinese Eastern Railroad. In September, 1932, Soviet Russia offered to sell the railroad, and, after a good deal of intermittent haggling, the matter was finally brought to a successful conclusion in 1935. In the following year the Japanese antagonized the U.S.S.R. by signing with Germany and Italy the Anti-Comintern Pact (November 25, 1936). Japan seems to have been induced to conclude this treaty because of a growing feeling of diplomatic isolation after she left the League. This feeling increased when she abrogated the Washington Naval Treaty (December, 1935), and, in January, 1936, walked out of the London Naval

Conference. The five-year agreement called for collabora-
tion in efforts to suppress communism. Additional secret
articles provided for consultation if the U.S.S.R. attacked
or threatened to attack any of the signatories and prohibited the conclusion of any political agreement with the
U.S.S.R. To retaliate, the U.S.S.R. refused to give the
Japanese long-term leases in the north Pacific fisheries
and, instead, drove hard annual bargains with them.

Toward the end of the decade, the Kwantung Army
essayed some passages at arms with the U.S.S.R. Far
Eastern Army. In July, 1938, they tried to occupy a spot
on the Manchukuo-Siberian border, Changkufeng, claimed
by the U.S.S.R. A large-scale battle developed and the
Japanese were forced to withdraw. In the early summer
of 1939, "Manchukuo" laid claim to some Outer Mongolian territory at Nomonhan and moved in troops.
Again there was a large-scale battle involving heavy
equipment. In the midst of the fighting came the astound-
ing news that Germany had concluded a non-aggression
pact with the U.S.S.R. Not willing to face the whole
strength of the U.S.S.R., the Japanese hastily settled the
incident. Despite the fact that by this action Germany
had violated the Anti-Comintern Pact, in September,
1940, Japan entered the Tripartite Pact. Her main object
was to secure German recognition for the New Order in
East Asia. This pact, which was to remain in force ten
years, provided that the signatories were to give full
assistance if one of them were "attacked by a Power at
present not involved in the European War or in the
Chinese-Japanese conflict." Subsequently, secret notes
were exchanged in which Germany agreed that a declaration of war did not automatically have to follow an
attack by a third Power and in which Germany promised
to aid Japan to secure a non-aggression pact with the
U.S.S.R. By direct order from Hitler the Japanese were
kept in ignorance of the intended German attack on
Russia. So on April 13, 1941, Matsuoka, the Foreign
Minister, signed a five-year Pact of Neutrality with the
U.S.S.R. Two months later the Germans were at war
with Russia.

The Japanese Move to the South. The main reason
the Japanese were anxious to obtain a Russian treaty was

to free themselves from fear of attack in the north while they exploited the opportunities the European War was opening up in Southeast Asia. On April 15, 1940, Foreign Minister Arita issued a statement stressing Japan's economic relations with the Netherlands East Indies and expressing concern as to their fate should the Netherlands become involved in the European War. The Dutch assured the Japanese that they would ask no other country to protect the Indies. On May 10, the Germans invaded the Netherlands. Ten days later Arita demanded that the Dutch Government agree to supply specified amounts of raw materials from the Indies. The Dutch evaded this demand, but in September, 1940, they were obliged to enter into extended economic discussions at Batavia with the Japanese. These talks lasted until June, 1941, the Dutch stubbornly refusing to give the Japanese what they wanted. Meanwhile, in June, 1940, Japan refused a United States request for a declaration that the *status quo* would be maintained in the Netherlands Indies.

The collapse of France in June, 1940, was immediately taken advantage of by the Japanese. Negotiations were simultaneously carried on in Hanoi and Tokyo. On August 30, 1940, the Vichy Government agreed to recognize Japanese predominance in the Far East and to aid Japan's war against China by permitting Japanese forces to be stationed in northern Indochina. The French officials in Indochina created some difficulties, but by the end of September the Japanese were in occupation. The Thai decided to profit from the situation by demanding the cession of certain border territories. The French refused and fighting broke out. The Japanese Government intervened and in March, 1941, forced a settlement on the two belligerents. This settlement included a secret protocol in which Indochina and Thailand undertook to make no agreement with a third Power which might endanger Japanese interests.

The United States and Japan Go to War. In 1940-41 the Japanese were anxious to achieve a successful termination of the China war, so that they might devote their full strength to their southern ventures. In both of these areas the prime obstacle was the United States, which had been lending material and moral support to the Chiang regime and encouraging the Dutch to resist Japanese demands. In the 1930's the United States had contented itself with a non-recognition doctrine for the changes made by war in East Asia. In July, 1938, however, the American Government established a "moral embargo" on shipments of war supplies to Japan and began to discourage extension of credits. In July, 1939, the United States abrogated the Japanese-American Commercial Treaty of 1911, and, when the one-year waiting period was up, instituted a system of licensing for the export to Japan of a variety of petroleum and metal products. The Japanese, beginning to feel the economic pinch, decided that if they were going to achieve their ends there would have to be some sort of an agreement with the United States.

In the spring of 1941, Admiral Nomura, the new Japanese ambassador to the United States, entered into conversations with Secretary of State Cordell Hull. The negotiations dragged on inconclusively until July, the main point at issue being the United States' insistence that Japan withdraw her troops from China and Indochina. Hull also wanted Japan to agree not to apply the Tripartite Pact to the United States. At an imperial conference held on July 2, 1941, the Japanese Government decided to carry out the plans it had been making with regard to Indochina even if it meant war with the United States and England. Consequently, preparations were made to move troops into southern Indochina. The United States, which had broken the Japanese communication code, learned of this decision through intercepts and on July 26, froze all Japanese assets. Similar action was taken by England and Canada, and the Netherlands East Indies Government announced special licenses would be needed for all trade. As a result, Japan suddenly had all her vital war materials imports cut off, but on July 29 she occupied southern Indochina.

On August 6, 1941, the Japanese submitted new proposals to the American Government. Japan promised to make no advance beyond Indochina, to leave Indochina when the China war was settled, and to guarantee the safety of the Philippines. In return she asked the United States to stop military preparations in the Far East, end the embargo, recognize Japan's position in Indochina, and bring pressure on Chiang K'ai-shek to end the China war. Two days later Hull rejected these conditions. Meanwhile, Prime Minister Konoe had sent an appeal to Roosevelt asking the President to meet with him. Roosevelt agreed to a meeting, but was later persuaded by Hull to postpone it until after an agreement had been concluded. On September 6, 1941, another imperial conference was held.

This meeting determined what Japan's minimum demands and maximum concessions would be, and decided that if, by the beginning of October, there was no hope of bringing the negotiations to a successful conclusion, the country should prepare for war. (*See Reading No. 12.*) On October 2, Hull handed the Japanese ambassador a note in which he expressed American dissatisfaction with the Japanese proposals made during September and suggested "that a clear-cut manifestation of Japan's intention in regard to the withdrawal of Japanese troops from China and French Indochina would be most helpful in making known . . . Japan's peaceful intentions. . . ." In Tokyo, General Tojo Hideki, the Army Minister, insisted this meant negotiations were at an end and war preparations should be made. Konoe opposed this proposal and still held out for continued talks. Even the Navy was reluctant to terminate negotiations with the United States. But the Army leaders argued that tropical weather conditions made it essential to strike before the winter was over. If Japan failed to act now, they said, she could do nothing for another year and by that time the embargo would have crippled her. (*See Reading No. 12.*) Konoe refused to accept the responsibility for plunging the nation into war, but was helpless in the face of Army demands. On October 16, 1941, he resigned and Tojo became Prime Minister (*See Reading No. 13.*) Final terms were sent to the ambassador in Washington, Nomura, who was soon joined by a special envoy, Kurusu Saburo. Nomura and Kurusu were warned that the Americans must accept these terms by November 25 (later extended to November 29) or ". . . things are automatically going to happen." Hull rejected the Japanese terms on November 26. On December 1 an imperial conference was held to ratify the decision to go to war. On December 2 the Japanese striking force, already at sea, was wirelessed orders to bomb Pearl Harbor.

The War in the Pacific. With the disaster at Pearl Harbor and the sinking of the British warships, the *Prince of Wales* and *Repulse* (December 10, 1941), Anglo-American naval power in the Pacific was too impaired to offer any obstacle to Japanese movements. From their bases in China, Indochina, Formosa, and the Pacific islands the Japanese fanned out in a wide arc. Everywhere the defenders were too few and the defenses too weak. In short order the Japanese completed the conquest of Hongkong (December 25, 1941), Malaya and Singapore (February 15, 1942), Burma (June, 1942), the Netherlands Indies (March, 1942), Manila (January 2, 1942), Bataan (April 9, 1942), and Corregidor (May 6, 1942). By the summer of 1942 Southeast Asia was theirs and they were reaching southward toward Australia and eastward toward Hawaii. Then they were brought to a halt by Australian and American troops in New Guinea and the Solomons (late 1942), and by American naval aviators at the Battle of Midway (3-6 June, 1942).

When the Japanese military leaders made their war plans in November, 1941, their intention had been quickly to seize southeast Asia and then to stand on the defensive. They expected that the United States and England would not be able to take any offensive counteraction for several years. They anticipated that they would have a period of time in which to organize the resources of their new conquests and develop enough economic and military strength to force their enemies to seek a compromise peace. There was also the chance that a German victory in Europe would knock out England and give the United States enough to worry about in the Atlantic. But the strength of the American economy permitted American military forces to develop the most tremendous striking power yet seen. By February, 1945, MacArthur had smashed his way up from New Guinea to Manila, and, shortly thereafter, Admiral Nimitz's Pacific island-hopping brought American forces to Okinawa (April-June 1945).

By 1945 Japan was no longer capable of sustaining her

war effort. The functioning of her economy depended upon imports of oil, coking coal, iron ore, bauxite, and a host of other materials, but American sea and air forces established such a tight blockade around the main Japanese islands that these imports were almost entirely cut off. By the end of the war Japan had lost about 95 per cent of her merchant shipping. Japanese production reached its peak in 1944 and then began a precipitous decline. As early as 1943 a peace movement had developed among senior Japanese statesmen such as Konoe, Wakatsuki, Hiranuma, and Okada. (*See Reading No. 14.*) However, it was not until the capture of Saipan that Tojo was forced out of office (July 18, 1944). He was succeeded by another Army general, Koiso Kuniaki. Koiso's Foreign Minister, Shigemitsu Mamoru, approached the Swedes as mediators, but before anything could be achieved the Koiso Cabinet was replaced by that of Admiral Suzuki Kantaro (April 7, 1945).

Suzuki, who had long been close to the Imperial Household, shared the Emperor's peace sentiments. He began to move in the direction of peace but had to be very careful to avoid an Army flare-up. On June 18, the Supreme War Council decided to ask the U.S.S.R. to act as a mediator. The Japanese desired to send Konoe to Moscow to discuss the matter, but on July 18, the Russians declined to receive Konoe. On July 26, the Potsdam Proclamation was issued by the United States, Great Britain, and China. It called upon Japan to surrender unconditionally or face "prompt and utter destruction." The Japanese Government was slow in responding to this demand. As a result the atom bomb was dropped on Hiroshima (August 6) and Nagasaki (August 9). In between the bombings, the U.S.S.R. entered the war and began to attack in Manchuria. Late on the night of August 9, an imperial conference was held to consider the acceptance of the Potsdam Proclamation. The military men wished to attach several conditions, but at the desire of the Emperor the proclamation was accepted with only the proviso that it include no "demand which prejudices the prerogatives of His Majesty as a Sovereign Ruler." The United States replied that from "the moment of surrender the authority of the Emperor and the Japanese

Government . . . shall be subject to the Supreme Commander of the Allied Powers." At the imperial conference which met on the morning of August 14, the Emperor, despite the continued opposition of the military, ordered the acceptance of the American offer. At noon the next day the surrender proclamation was broadcast to the nation. On August 30, the Americans began to arrive, and on September 2, the formal surrender ceremony was held aboard the *Missouri* in Tokyo Bay.

> The summer grasses!
> All that is left of the
> warriors' dream.
>
> BASHO (1644-1694)

— 4 —

OCCUPATION AND AFTER

Structure of the Occupation. The Occupation of Japan was from start to finish an American operation. Stalin had originally wanted a Russian general to share equally in the responsibility, but, on August 12, 1945, he finally agreed to the appointment of General Douglas MacArthur as the sole Supreme Commander for the Allied Powers (SCAP). Later, at the Moscow Conference of Foreign Ministers (December, 1945), it was decided to establish an eleven-nation Far Eastern Commission and a Four-Power Allied Council for Japan. The Far Eastern Commission, which had its headquarters in Washington, was empowered to formulate policy and to review the actions of SCAP. The Allied Council for Japan, consisting of delegates from the United States (SCAP or his deputy), the U.S.S.R., China, and the British Commonwealth, met in Tokyo and was a purely advisory and consultative body. Neither of these agencies had much influence on Occupation policy, which developed in the main out of the *United States Initial Post-Surrender Policy for Japan* (August 29, 1945) and the *Basic Initial Post-Surrender Directive* (November 8, 1945). The latter of these documents cited as the ultimate objective of the Occupation the fostering of "conditions which will give the greatest possible assurance that Japan will not again become a menace to the peace and security of the world and will permit her eventual admission as a responsible and peaceful member of the family of nations." It was desirable "that the Japanese Government conform as closely as may be to principles of democratic self-government," but it was "not the responsibility of the Occupation forces to impose on Japan any form of government not supported by the freely expressed will of the people." At the outset of the Occupation the shortage of military government personnel led to the basic decision that SCAP would not institute direct control of the Japanese people but would retain the Japanese Government and act through it.

Liquidating Japanese Imperialism. The first step taken by the Occupation was to limit Japanese sovereignty to the four main islands of Hokkaido, Honshu, Shikoku, and Kyushu "and such minor islands as may be determined." In accordance with the Cairo Declaration (November, 1943) Japan was immediately stripped of the Pacific mandated islands, Korea, Manchuria, Formosa, and the Pescadores. The United States took the Ryukyu Islands (Okinawa) under its direct administration, and in April, 1947, was given the strategic trusteeship of Japan's Pacific islands. In the north Soviet Russia, acting under the terms of the Yalta Agreement (February, 1945), took possession of the Kurile Islands and southern Sakhalin.

The second task undertaken was the destruction of Japan's war potential. The Army and Navy Ministries were abolished, and the Army and Navy disbanded. Six and a half million Japanese sailors, soldiers, and ·civilians were repatriated from overseas. All munitions and military equipment were confiscated and destroyed. All existing aircraft were destroyed and manufacture of any type of aircraft was forbidden. Factories producing war materials were closed down if they could not be converted to civilian use. Scientific research related to military uses was prohibited. It was planned eventually to remove entirely certain industries, for example, synthetic oils, and severely limit others, such as steel and machine tools.

As soon as the Occupation began, arrests were made of suspected war criminals. In January, 1946, SCAP set up a special International Military Tribunal for the Far East, to which it presented twenty-eight Japanese leaders for trial. Hearings were finished in April, 1948, but the judgment was not rendered until November, 1948. Tojo and six others were condemned to hang. Of the others, sixteen received life sentences, one twenty years, and one seven years. Two of the defendants had died and one had become insane. Besides this major trial, the various Allies each tried Japanese accused of ordinary crimes against the laws and customs of war and against humanity. In all about 4,200 Japanese were found guilty, 700 being executed. The American trials were finally completed in October, 1949. In addition to bringing to justice those guilty of war atrocities, SCAP endeavored wherever possible to recover looted property and return it to its rightful owners.

Democratization Measures.   One of the first acts of the Occupation was to order the Japanese Government to free all political prisoners and grant full freedom of speech and press to the Japanese people. In order to remove undemocratic influences, SCAP, on January 4, 1946, directed the Japanese Government to suppress all ultranationalist, paramilitary, anti-foreign, and terrorist organizations. The same order established certain categories of persons who were to be prohibited from engaging in public affairs. As a result of this order about 186,000 people were "purged." A year later the purge was extended to the fields of local government, cultural activities, and economic life. On April 10, 1946, a new Diet was elected under a revised election law which gave the vote to women and lowered the voting age from 25 to 20 years. Seventy-two percent of the eligible voters cast their ballots.

As early as the fall of 1945 the Japanese Government,

at the instigation of SCAP, began work on a new constitution. Its suggestions proved too conservative for the Occupation officials, who thereupon prepared a draft constitution of their own. The present Japanese Constitution is largely based on this SCAP draft. (*See Reading No. 15.*) To make sure that at a later date no charges of illegality would be levied at the Constitution, the Japanese Government carefully followed the amendment procedure laid down in the Meiji Constitution.

The Constitution, which went into effect May 3, 1947, carefully proclaims that "soverign power resides with the people," and that the "Emperor shall be the symbol of the State . . . deriving his position from the will of the people." The people exercise their sovereignty through the Diet which is "the highest organ of State power." The Diet consists of a House of Representatives, whose members have a four-year term, and a House of Councillors, whose members serve for six years. The lower house is supreme. By a two-thirds vote it can pass any law over the opposition of the Councillors, and, in the event of a difference of opinion over the budget, the decision of the House of Representatives is final. The Prime Minister is designated from among the members of either house. Here again, if there is a difference of opinion, that of the lower house prevails. Once the Prime Minister has been named, he appoints and removes the other members of the Cabinet at will, the only restriction being that a majority must be from the lower house. If the House of Representatives passes a non-confidence resolution the Cabinet has to resign or dissolve the house and hold a general election.

A detailed bill of "eternal and inviolate rights" running to thirty-one articles is included in the Constitution. Another interesting feature is the enhanced status of the judiciary, which under the old system had been an appointive service under the Justice Minister. A Supreme Court, consisting of a chief judge and several associate judges, is given the power to determine the constitutionality of all laws, orders, and acts, and also is given complete control over the operation and administration of the courts. Supreme Court judges are appointed by the Cabinet, but at the next House of Representatives election and every ten years thereafter this appointment must be reviewed by the voters. Inferior court judges are appointed by the Cabinet for ten-year terms from among candidates nominated by the Supreme Court.

The most controversial article in the Constitution was inserted by General MacArthur himself—the famous Article 9, in which war or the use of force is renounced and "land, sea, and air forces, as well as other war potential" are forbidden to be maintained. This has proved to be embarrassing to both the American and Japanese Governments. Any change in the Constitution must first be approved by two-thirds of all the members of each house and then be submitted to a popular referendum.

In addition to giving a more democratic structure to the central government, the Occupation also instituted reforms aimed at making local government more responsive to public feeling. The prefectural governships and other local offices were made elective and the legislative branch of the local governments was given wider authority. The police system was decentralized and placed under elected local police commissions, though places too small to afford a force were allowed to use a rural police force organized by the central government.

It seemed fundamental to the Occupation authorities that changes in political institutions must be backed by social and educational changes. The Japanese law codes were revised to give women equality with men in all respects. The basic unit recognized by Japanese law was changed from the "household" to the individual. The period of compulsory education was extended from six years to nine years and a large measure of control over the educational system was put in the hands of elected local school boards. Textbooks were revised to eliminate ultranationalist bias and the teaching of "morals" was banned. On December 15, 1945, the Japanese Government was ordered to end all State support of Shinto shrines and to halt the teaching of Shinto in the schools. In the future there was to be no compulsory participation in Shinto ritual and no propagation of the idea that the Japanese ruler was superior to other rulers or the Japanese superior to other peoples. In a rescript issued on

January 1, 1946, the Emperor repudiated the conception that he was divine or that the Japanese people were destined to rule the world.

Economic Reforms. American planners were convinced that the tenancy system, the absence of a well-developed union movement, and the existence of huge monopolistic business combines, such as the *Zaibatsu*, had been among the factors contributing to Japanese aggression. They endeavored, therefore, to remedy all three. In October, 1946, the Diet passed a Land Reform Law. By its terms all non-resident landowners were to sell all their land and resident owners were to sell all land over 2.45 acres (in Hokkaido, 9.80 acres) to an elected local land commission, which would in turn sell it to landless farmers. Since the price was fixed in terms of the pre-inflation values of 1939, the reform amounted to an expropriation of the landowning class. The purchasers were allowed thirty years in which to pay. By 1952, 5,000,000 acres had changed hands, and 90 per cent of the farm land was owned by the persons cultivating it. To protect the tenants who remained, a Tenancy Law fixed rents at 25 per cent of the rice crop and 15 per cent of other crops. Additional security was assured by requiring written leases. While this reform was important, the basic problem still remained—too many farmers for too little land.

As early as December, 1945, the Occupation arranged the passage of a Trade Union Law giving workers the right to join unions, to bargain collectively, and to strike. Unions grew rapidly, their membership increasing between 1946 and 1948 from 496,000 to 6,636,710—about half of the non-agricultural workers. In time, labor-union activities became a little too exuberant even for SCAP. Consequently, in September, 1946, the Japanese Government was allowed to pass a law prohibiting government employees from striking and limiting the right to strike of public utilities workers. The Government was permitted to classify as a public utility any enterprise necessary to the people's daily livelihood.

Early in the Occupation, steps were taken to freeze all *Zaibatsu* assets. In April, 1946, a Holding Company Liquidation Commission was established. Over eighty-three holding companies turned over all their assets to this commission, receiving in return non-negotiable ten-year bonds. The Japanese Government endeavored to sell these securities to the general public in the hope of creating a more widespread ownership of industry. It apparently did not succeed in this purpose, for in March, 1951, a survey revealed that 8.32 per cent of the stock-owners held 68.13 per cent of all the shares. To eliminate the influence of *Zaibatsu* personnel there was an economic purge in January, 1947. Later the same year a law was passed forbidding members of *Zaibatsu* families to be associated with any of their former enterprises for a ten-year period. In 1947 an Anti-Monopoly Law and an Economic Deconcentration Law were also passed. Finally, in July, 1948, a Trade Association Law prohibiting eighteen unfair practices went into effect. Much of the wartime profits of the *Zaibatsu* were recovered in 1946 by a capital-levy tax.

Shift in America's Attitude Toward Japan. In 1946 the Pauley Report on Reparations advocated the whole-sale transfer of a great portion of Japan's industrial plant to other Asiatic countries. It seemed to forecast a sub-sistence economy for Japan. However, Soviet Russia's refusal to classify her Manchurian booty as reparations delayed the implementation of this plan. Soon the development of the cold war, the failure of China to assume her expected role in East Asia, and concern over the cost to America of subsidizing the Japanese economy led the United States Government to revise its attitude.

The first sign of change came in May, 1947, in a speech by Under Secretary of State Dean Acheson, in which he spoke of making Japan the workshop of Asia. In the spring of 1948, a series of reports was made by various American missions to Japan advocating the establishment of a strong industrial Japan and recommending against the transfer of machinery. SCAP began to take a more active interest in Japanese economic policies. In 1949 a severe austerity program designed to place the Japanese economy back on its feet was instituted under the direction of Joseph M. Dodge. Until the Korean War (June 25, 1950) the American purpose in Japan was merely to strengthen the economy, so that there would be no social unrest for communists to exploit. After the Korean War the United States, concerned with Japan as a military factor, permitted the establishment of what was in effect an embryonic army.

Political Developments under the Occupation. In September, 1945, political parties again came to life in Japan. The left-wing elements, excluding the communists, organized the Social Democratic Party, while the conservative politicians established the Liberal Party and the Progressive Party. The difference between the two conservative groups was not so much in policy as in personalities and political traditions. The Liberal Party may be considered a lineal descendant of the old *Seiyukai;* the Progressive Party, of the *Minseito.* In the April, 1946, election the Liberals won a plurality. It was expected that their leader, Hatoyama Ichiro, would become Prime Minister, but at the last minute SCAP purged him, his place being taken by his lieutenant, Yoshida Shigeru, a former career diplomat. Before the next election (April, 1947), a group of Liberals deserted Yoshida and joined with the Progressives to form the Democratic Party. The Social Democrats emerged from the election as the ranking party. On May 24, 1947, the Socialist leader, Katayama Tetsu, organized a coalition cabinet with the support of the Democratic Party. In February, 1948, a split over financial policies developed among the Social Democrats and Katayama resigned. Ashida Hitoshi, the president of the Democratic Party, became Prime Minister with Socialist support. This cabinet had to resign in October, 1948, as the result of the revelation of political corruption scandals involving its members. Once again Yoshida was called upon to assume control of the Government. The following January new elections were held. The Liberal Party won an overwhelming victory, obtaining 264 seats out of a possible 466. The Social Democratic Party declined from 144 to 49 seats and the Democratic Party lost about half its representation. For the rest of the Occupation, Yoshida was firmly in power.

The Japanese Communist Party. In the fall of 1945 the Japanese Communist Party, reconstituted under leaders who had spent the 1930's in jail or abroad, once again began political activity. At first they adopted a program of "peaceful revolution" and consequently made substantial headway in the unions and with the electorate. In the elections of 1946 and 1947 they won four or five seats in the House of Representatives, receiving about 3 to 4 per cent of the vote. In January, 1949, the Communist Party elected thirty-five representatives, polling about 3,000,000 votes, or almost 10 per cent of the vote. A year later, in January, 1950, the Cominform criticized the JCP's policies and in the spring of 1950 there was a switch to a program of "militant obstructionism." In June, 1950, SCAP purged forty-one Communist Party leaders and banned *Red Flag*, the Communist Party publication. The Japanese Government also purged suspected Communists from its employ. In the spring and summer of 1952 there were several serious Communist-inspired anti-American riots. This policy of violence alienated many Japanese and in subsequent elections the JCP has only received about 2 per cent of the vote. In February, 1954, the Japanese Government estimated there were about 100,000 JCP members.

The Peace Treaty. On September 8, 1951, forty-eight nations concluded a peace treaty with Japan. Three nations which had attended the conference—U.S.S.R., Czechoslovakia, and Poland—refused to sign the treaty. India and Burma did not attend, preferring to make their own treaties. The treaty, which was largely of American origin, was an "act of reconciliation." (*See Reading No. 16.*) The Japanese agreed to the territorial changes which the Allies had made. In addition, they agreed to an American trusteeship in Okinawa and the Bonins. All the rights Japan had acquired in China were renounced, as were also any claims on the Antarctic. No economic restrictions were imposed, but Japan agreed to enter into reparation negotiations with any signatory who wished to do so. It was recognized that Japan "possessed the inherent right of individual or collective self-defense," and she was specifically authorized to conclude agreements for the stationing of foreign troops on her territory. On the same day the peace treaty was signed, the United States and Japan concluded a security treaty which allowed the United States to station military forces in Japan and obligated her to defend Japan. (*See Reading No. 17.*)

Japan's Economic Problems. In January, 1955, Japan had a population of over eighty-eight millions. Although the birth-rate is lower than that of the United States, the population is growing at the rate of a million a year. Japan's fundamental economic problem is the feeding of her people. Japanese food resources are not sufficient to do this, and more than one-fifth of the food supply must be imported annually. To pay for these food imports Japan must export manufactures. But here again, because of the poverty of her natural resources, Japan must import the raw materials required by her export industries.

In the postwar period several factors have made it difficult for Japan to balance her imports with her exports. First, there is the matter of price. Improved labor conditions, the difficulty of depressing these conditions because of labor's political power, and inflationary pressures have tended to keep Japanese export prices above those of the rest of the world. In addition, world textile markets are shrinking as underdeveloped countries initiate their industrialization, and Japan is being forced to shift her exports into fields where the cost of raw materials imports is the highest—the heavy industries. Moreover, there is the problem of the trade and money controls which are in force in almost all countries. Consequently, Japan has had an import excess every year since the war's end. This deficit has been met year after year by one form or another of United States aid, which, between September, 1945, and April, 1952, amounted to $2,000,-000,000. In addition to outright aid, there are also the official and private American purchases which have been made in Japan.

Even under the Occupation an attempt had been made to deal with this problem by the economies of the Dodge program. During the first two years of restored sovereignty these measures were relaxed, but in the fall of 1953 the Yoshida Cabinet launched an austerity program designed to cut prices and reduce the amount of goods diverted into the domestic market. The Hatoyama Cabinet has continued this policy. The feeling has also been growing among business and governmental circles that Japan's economic margin is too narrow to afford the luxury of domestic economic competition. In 1949 the Anti-monopoly Law was revised and a definition of competition inserted which made the Law a dead letter. After 1951 a number of business combinations began to emerge, linked by ex-*Zaibatsu* personnel and by common relations with the four or five largest banks. In 1952 the Diet removed the ban on the use of *Zaibatsu* names and many companies have now resumed their old names. In 1953 the Anti-monopoly Law was again revised and cartels made legal.

Japanese Politics Since the Occupation. In October, 1951, the Japanese Diet ratified the Peace Treaty and Security Pact; on April 28, 1952, Japan regained her full sovereignty. Five months later, October 1, 1952, the first post-Occupation Diet election was held. Since the last election in 1949 two important political changes had occurred. The first was the division of the Social Democrats into the Right Social Democrats and the Left Social Democrats. This split took place in the fall of 1951 as a result of differences over the policy to be adopted toward the peace arrangements. The Right Social Democrats rejected the Security Pact but accepted the Peace Treaty; the Left rejected both. The second was the return of the purgees to political activity. In October, 1950, 10,000 persons were depurged; in June, 1951, 69,000. Many of these men immediately returned to influence in the political parties. One paroled war criminal, Shigemitsu Mamoru, even became president of a reorganized version of the old Democratic Party called the Progressive Party. Prime Minister Yoshida's Liberal Party won a bare majority in the election, 139 of its 242 elected representatives being purgees.

Among the new Liberal representatives was Hatoyama Ichiro. The feeling arose among some members of the Liberal Party that Yoshida should resign in favor of his former chief. However, Yoshida refused to do this. The Hatoyama faction of the Liberal Party was the difference between Yoshida having and not having a Diet majority. This was demonstrated in March, 1953, when their abstention from voting permitted the opposition parties to push a non-confidence resolution through the Diet.

Yoshida dissolved the Diet and held new elections in April. This election reduced his majority to a plurality and made his continuation in office dependent upon the votes of a dissident group of former Liberals.

That these conservative differences are more a matter of personalities rather than of policies was shown by the way all conservatives rallied behind the Yoshida cabinet when the rearmament issue came to the fore in the spring of 1954. It will be recalled that the Japanese Constitution forbade the maintenance of military forces. Nevertheless, in July, 1950, a 75,000-man National Police Reserve had been set up. In August, 1952, this had been increased in size and renamed the Japan Safety Corps. In the spring of 1954 a Mutual Security Assistance Pact, which had been concluded between Japan and the United States, came before the Diet for ratification. The two branches of the Social Democrats were utterly opposed to this pact, but the Diet approved it on April 28, and then passed implementing laws creating Ground, Air, and Sea Self-Defense Corps numbering about 150,000 men. These forces were placed under a civilian head, but the higher officers were, to a large extent, former members of the old Imperial Army and Navy. At about the same time these measures were adopted, the Diet also passed a new police law, which placed all police under a National Police Board and gave the central government the right to appoint police chiefs for prefectures and large cities.

In the fall of 1954 the Yoshida-Hatoyama quarrel came to a head when a number of Liberals seceded and joined with the Progressive Party to form the Japan Democratic Party. Yoshida, seeing the inevitability of a vote of non-confidence, resigned on December 9, 1954, and turned the presidency of the Liberal Party over to Ogata Taketora. The Social Democrats voted with the Japan Democratic Party to designate Hatoyama as a caretaker Prime Minister until elections could be held. The results of the February, 1955, elections gave Hatoyama only 185 representatives, about fifty votes short of a majority. When the Diet met in March, the Liberal Party, which had obtained 112 seats, voted to support Hatoyama; hence he remained as Prime Minister. The election platform of

the Japan Democratic Party foreshadowed additional
changes to be made in the Occupation reforms, but as yet
these changes have not been made.

In foreign policy Hatoyama seems determined to continue Japan's ties with the United States. But he also feels
it would be in Japan's interest to resume relations with
the U.S.S.R. and Communist China. In this he reflects a
sentiment widespread among all circles of Japanese that
a resumption of trade with Communist China will help
solve Japan's pressing economic problems. To the Japanese the issue is purely economic and does not involve
any ideological surrender. The basic temper of Japan is
still conservative. In none of the postwar elections have
the conservative parties failed to receive over 60 per cent
of the vote cast. Changes will occur, but they will in all
probability be along the lines of a return to the traditional.

Part II

READINGS

EDICT CLOSING JAPAN, 1636[1]

At the time this edict was issued the Tokugawa were still willing to maintain trading contracts with the Portuguese. The edict had two main objectives: (1) to cut off communications between dissident political elements in Japan and the samurai who had fled abroad; and (2) to prevent "Kirishitan" (Christian) missionaries from entering the country. To accomplish these ends, strict controls were placed on the activities of the traders. "Bateren" is the Japanese term for the Jesuit fathers. "Ito-wappu" refers to the bulk purchasing of silk by the silk guilds.

1. No Japanese ships may leave for foreign countries.
2. No Japanese may go abroad secretly. If anybody tries to do this, he will be killed, and the ship and owner(s) will be placed under arrest whilst higher authority is informed.
3. Any Japanese now living abroad who tries to return to Japan will be put to death.
4. If any *Kirishitan* believer is discovered, you two [Nagasaki *Bugyo*] will make a full investigation.
5. Any informer(s) revealing the whereabouts of a *bateren* will be paid 200 or 300 pieces of silver. If any other categories of *Kirishitans* are discovered, the informer(s) will be paid at your discretion as hitherto.
6. On the arrival of foreign ships, arrangements will be made to have them guarded by ships provided by the

[1] C. R. Boxer, *The Christian Century in Japan, 1549-1650* (University of California Press, Berkeley, 1951), pp. 439-40. Used by permission of the Publisher.

Omura clan whilst report is being made to Yedo, as hitherto.

7. Any foreigners who help the *bateren* or other criminal foreigners will be imprisoned at Omura as hitherto.

8. Strict search will be made for *bateren* on all incoming ships.

9. No offspring of Southern Barbarians will be allowed to remain. Anyone violating this order will be killed, and all relatives punished according to the gravity of the offence.

10. If any Japanese have adopted the offspring of Southern Barbarians they deserve to die. Nevertheless, such adopted children and their foster-parents will be handed over to the Southern Barbarians for deportation.

11. If any deportees should try to return or to communicate with Japan by letter or otherwise, they will of course be killed if they are caught, whilst their relatives will be severely dealt with, according to the gravity of the offence.

12. *Samurai* are not allowed to have direct commercial dealings with either foreign or Chinese shipping at Nagasaki.

13. Nobody other than those of the five places (Yedo, Kyoto, Osaka, Sakai, and Nagasaki) is allowed to participate in the allocation of *ito-wappu* and the fixing of silk import prices.

14. Purchases can only be made after the *ito-wappu* is fixed. However, as the Chinese ships are small, you will not be too rigorous with them. Only twenty days are allowed for the sale.

15. The twentieth day of the ninth month is the deadline for the return of foreign ships, but latecomers will be allowed fifty days grace from the date of their arrival. Chinese ships will be allowed to leave a little after the departure of the [Portuguese] galliots.

16. Unsold goods cannot be left in charge of Japanese for storage or safekeeping.

17. Representatives of the five [shogunal] cities should arrive at Nagasaki not later than the fifth day of the long month. Late arrivals will not be allowed to participate in the silk allocation and purchase.

18. Ships arriving at Hirado will not be allowed to transact business until after the price allocations have been fixed at Nagasaki.

Nineteenth day of the fifth month of the thirteenth year of Kwanei [*June 22, 1636*].

Addressed to Sakakibara Hida-no-kami and Baba Saburozayemon, the joint *bugyo* of Nagasaki, and signed by Hotta Kaga-no-kami, Abe Bungo-no-kami, Saki Sanuki-no-kami and Doi Oi-no-suké, the four great councillors or *Go-roju*.

— Reading No. 2 —

THE CHARTER OATH, 1868[2]

The Emperor Meiji announced this oath to the nation's ancestral gods and goddesses in an ancient ritual. The political history of Japan down to 1889 largely revolved around arguments as to the exact ways in which this document was to be interpreted and applied. The immediate purpose of the oath was to quiet public opinion and give the Government a chance to organize itself.

1. We will call councils and rule the nation according to public opinion.
2. Men of the upper and lower classes shall without distinction be united in all enterprises.
3. Civil officials and military officials shall be in one accord and all the common people shall be so treated that they can attain their aims and feel no discontent.
4. Old unworthy ways and customs shall be destroyed

[2] *The Japan Year Book, 1939-1940* (Tokyo, 1939), p. 83, slightly modified.

and everything shall be based upon the just and equitable principles of nature.

5. Knowledge shall be sought among the nations of the world and thus the welfare of the Empire will be promoted.

— Reading No. 3 —

MEMORIAL FOR THE ESTABLISHMENT OF A REPRESENTATIVE ASSEMBLY, 1874[3]

This document, which was submitted to the Government on January 17, 1874, reveals the extent to which Western political ideas had begun to penetrate Japanese thought. But it also shows the continuance of traditional Japanese values, for the strongest argument the petitioners advance in favor of an assembly is that "then the people of the whole country will be of one mind" and the country will become strong.

When we humbly reflect upon the quarter in which the governing power lies, we find that it lies not with the Crown (the Imperial House) on the one hand, nor with the people on the other, but with the officials alone. We do not deny that the officials respect the Crown, and yet the Crown is gradually losing its prestige, nor do we

[3] Reprinted from the *Japan Weekly Mail* in W. W. McLaren, ed., *Japanese Government Documents, Transactions of the Asiatic Society of Japan,* 42, 1 (Tokyo, 1914), pp. 427-33.

deny that they protect the people, and yet the manifold decrees of the government appear in the morning and are changed in the evening, the administration is conducted in an arbitrary manner, rewards and punishments are prompted by partiality, the channel by which the people should communicate with the government is blocked up and they cannot state their grievances. Is it to be hoped that the empire can be perfectly ruled in this manner? An infant knows that it cannot be done. We fear, therefore, that if a reform is not effected the state will be ruined. Unable to resist the promptings of our patriotic feelings, we have sought to devise a means of rescuing it from this danger, and we find it to consist in developing public discussion in the empire. The means of developing public discussion is the establishment of a council-chamber chosen by the people. Then a limit will be placed to the power of the officials, and both governors and governed will obtain peace and prosperity. We ask leave then to make some remarks on this subject.

The people whose duty it is to pay taxes to the government possesses the right of sharing in their government's affairs and of approving or condemning. This being a principle universally acknowledged it is not necessary to waste words in discussing it. We therefore humbly pray that the officials will not resist this great truth. Those who just now oppose the establishment of a council-chamber chosen by the people say: "Our people are wanting in culture and intelligence, and have not yet advanced into the region of enlightenment. It is too early yet to establish a council-chamber elected by the people." If it really be as they say, then the way to give to the people culture and intelligence and to cause them to advance swiftly into the region of enlightenment is to establish a council-chamber chosen by the people.

For in order to give our people culture and intelligence and to cause them to advance into the region of enlightenment, they must in the first place be induced to protect their rights, to respect and value themselves, and be inspired by a spirit of sympathy with the griefs and joys of the empire, which can only be done by giving them a voice in its concerns. It has never happened that under such circumstances the people have been content to

remain in a backward condition or have been satisfied
with want of culture and intelligence. To expect that they
shall acquire culture and intelligence by themselves and
advance by themselves into regions of enlightenment is
like "waiting a hundred years for the water to clear."
The worst argument they put forward is that to establish
a council-chamber at once would be simply to assemble
all the blockheads in the empire.

What shocking self-conceit and arrogant contempt
for the people this indicates! No doubt there are among
the officials men who surpass others in intelligence and
ingenuity, but how do they know that society does not
contain men who surpass them in intelligence and
knowledge? Whence it may be inferred that the people of
the empire are not to be treated with such arrogant contempt. If again they deserve to be treated with arrogant
contempt, are the officials themselves not a part of the
nation, in which case they also are wanting in intelligence
and culture? Between the arbitrary decisions of a few
officials and the general opinion of the people, as ascer-
tained by public discussion, where is the balance of
wisdom or stupidity?

We believe that the intelligence of the officials must
have made progress as compared with what it was
previous to the Restoration, for the intelligence and
knowledge of human beings increase in proportion as
they are exercised. Therefore to establish a council-
chamber chosen by the people would promote the culture and intelligence of the people and cause them to
advance rapidly into the region of enlightenment. The
duty of a government and the object which it ought to
promote in the fulfillment of that duty is to enable the
people to make progress. Consequently in uncivilized
ages, when manners were barbarous and people fierce,
turbulent and unaccustomed to obey, it was of course
the duty of the government to teach them to obey, but
our country is now no longer uncivilized, and the tract-
ableness of our people is already excessive. The object
which our government ought therefore to promote is by
the establishment of a council-chamber chosen by the
people to arouse in them a spirit of enterprise, and to
enable them to comprehend the duty of participating in

the burdens of the empire and sharing in the direction of its affairs, and then the people of the whole country will be of one mind.

How is the government to be made strong? It is by the people of the empire becoming of one mind. We will not prove this by quoting ancient historical facts. We will show it by the change in our government of October last. How great was the peril! What is the reason of our government standing isolated? How many of the people of the empire rejoiced at or grieved over the change in the government of October last? Not only was there neither grief nor joy on account of it, but eight or nine out of every ten in the empire were utterly ignorant that it had taken place, and they were only surprised at the disbanding of the troops. The establishment of a council-chamber chosen by the people will create community of feeling between the government and the people, and they will mutually unite into one body. Then and only then will the country become strong.

We have now proved our position by universal principles, by the actual political state of our country, by the duty of a government and by the change which occurred in our government last October. Our belief in the justice of our views is strengthened, and we are firmly of the opinion that the only way to develop and maintain the destinies of the empire is to establish a council-chamber chosen by the people to develop public discussion among them. We will not here enlarge upon the manner in which the idea is to be wrought out, as that would occupy too much space.

We are informed that the present officials, under the pretence of being conservative, are generally averse to progress, and they nickname those who advocate reforms as "rash progressives," and oppose their opinions with the two words "too early." We ask leave to make an explanation here.

In the first place we do not comprehend the phrase "rash progression." If by rash progression is meant measures which are heedlessly initiated, then it is a council-chamber chosen by the people that will remedy this heedlessness. Do you mean by "rash progression" the want of harmony between the different branches of the

administration, and the postponement of urgent matters
to the less urgent in a period of reform, so that the
measures carried out are wanting in unity of plan? The
cause of this is the want of a fixed law in the country, and
the fact that the officials proceed according to the bent of
their own inclinations. The existence of these two things
proves the necessity for establishing a council-chamber
chosen by the people. Progress is the most beautiful
thing in the world, and is the law of all things moral and
physical. Men actuated by principle cannot condemn
this word progress, but their condemnation must be intended for the word "rash," but the word "rash" has no
connection with a council-chamber chosen by the people.

We are not only unable to comprehend what the words
"too early" have to do with a council-chamber elected
by the people, but our opinion is directly the opposite
of what this phrase expresses. For if a council-chamber
chosen by the people were established to-day, we may
fairly suppose that it would not be expected to be in
complete working order until many months or years had
elapsed. We are only afraid therefore of a single day's
delay in establishing it, and therefore we say that we
hold the exact opposite of this opinion.

Another argument of the officials is that the council-
chambers now existing in European and American states
were not formed in a day, but were only brought into
their present state by gradual progress, and therefore we
cannot to-day copy them suddenly. But gradual progress
has not been the case with council-chambers only; all
branches of knowledge and science and art are subject to
the same conditions. The reason why foreigners have
perfected this only after the lapse of centuries, is that
no examples existed previously and these had to be discovered by actual experience. If we can select examples
from them and adopt their contrivances, why should we
not be successful in working them out? If we are to delay
the using of steam machinery until we have discovered
the principles of steam for ourselves, or to wait till we
have discovered the principles of electricity before we
construct an electric telegraph, our government will be
unable to set to work.

Our object in seeking to prove that a council-chamber

elected by the people ought to-day to be established in our country, and that the degree of progress amongst the people of this country is sufficient for the establishment of such a council-chamber, is not to prevent the officials from making use of various pretexts for opposing it, but we are animated by the desire that by establishing such a council-chamber public discussion in the empire may be established, the spirit of the empire be roused to activity, the affection between governors and governed be made greater, sovereign and subject be brought to love each other, our imperial country be maintained and its destinies be developed, and prosperity and peace be assured to all. We shall esteem ourselves fortunate if you will adopt our suggestions.

The Government's Reply

With respect to the memorial presented by Soyejima, a Samurai of Saga-ken and seven others, upon the subject of the establishment of a council-chamber chosen by the people, the principle is an excellent one, and this college having received sanction to a similar proposal made by itself, has drafted a set of regulations. The suggestion, therefore, will be adopted. At the same time, in view of the instructions issued last year to the Fu and Ken, with respect to Local Assemblies, and the fact that the Home Office has just been constituted, we recommend to the Council of State (*Sei-in*) that the Home Office shall be called upon to give its opinion, and that after the Local Assemblies shall have been opened, the question of a council-chamber chosen by the people shall then be taken up.

RESCRIPT PROMISING A PARLIAMENT, 1881 [4]

The effect of this rescript was to remove the question of a parliament from the political arena and give the Government a breathing space in which to look to its defenses. Once the Emperor had announced that he was considering the matter, it was difficult to discuss it without running the risk of being disrespectful toward him. This aspect of the edict was reinforced by the Emperor's warning against agitation for sudden changes.

We, sitting on the Throne which has been occupied by Our dynasty for over 2500 years, and now exercising in Our name and right all authority and power transmitted to us by Our ancestors, have long had in view gradually to establish a constitutional form of government, to the end that Our successors on the Throne may be provided with a rule for their guidance.

It was with this object in view that in the 8th year of Meiji We established the Senate, and in the 11th year of Meiji authorized the formation of Local Assemblies, thus laying the foundation for the gradual reforms which we contemplated. These Our acts must convince you, Our subjects, of Our determination in this respect from the beginning.

Systems of government differ in different countries, but sudden and unusual changes cannot be made without great inconvenience.

Our ancestors in Heaven watch Our acts, and We recognise Our responsibility to them for the faithful discharge of Our high duties, in accordance with the princi-

[4] Reprinted from the *Japan Weekly Mail* in McLaren, *op. cit.*, pp. 86-87.

ples, and the perpetual increase of the glory, they have bequeathed to Us.

We therefore hereby declare that We shall, in the 23rd year of Meiji, establish a Parliament, in order to carry into full effect the determination We have announced, and We charge Our faithful subjects bearing Our commissions to make, in the mean time, all necessary preparations to that end.

With regard to the limitations upon the Imperial prerogative, and the constitution of the Parliament, We shall decide hereafter and make proclamation in due time.

We perceive that the tendency of Our people is to advance too rapidly, and without that thought and consideration which alone can make progress enduring, and We warn Our subjects, high and low, to be mindful of Our will, and that those who may advocate sudden and violent changes, thus disturbing the peace of Our realm, will fall under Our displeasure.

We expressly proclaim this to Our subjects.

— Reading No. 5 —

IMPERIAL PRECEPTS TO THE SOLDIERS AND SAILORS, 1882 [5]

This document has several points of interest. First, there is the official version of Japanese history with which it opens. Second, there is the insistence upon the principle that the Emperor retains supreme command of the military forces. The context shows that this was originally intended to preclude any military commander from assert-

[5] *The Japan Year Book, 1939-1940* (Tokyo, 1939), pp. 207-09.

ing his independence. Yet, at a later time, it was used to justify the independence of the military from the civil authorities. Third, there is the attempt to create an ethical code for the military, stressing loyalty, obedience, courage, simplicity, and faithfulness. These precepts were issued only five years after a former commander-in-chief of the Imperial Army, Saigo Takamori, had revolted against the Government. Many Army officers "faithful in small matters," that is, seduced by their personal loyalty to Saigo, had followed him out of the Army, nearly wrecking it. This document was periodically read to Japanese soldiers and sailors. On at least one occasion a Japanese officer committed suicide because he had made an error while reading it.

The forces of Our Empire are in all ages under the command of the Emperor. It is more than twenty-five centuries since the Emperor Jimmu, leading in person the soldiers of the Otomo and Mononobé clans, subjected the unruly tribes of the land and ascended the Imperial Throne to rule over the whole country. During this period the military system has undergone frequent changes in accordance with those in the state of society. In ancient times the rule was that the Emperor should take personal command of the forces; and although the military authority was sometimes delegated to the Empress or to the Prince Imperial, it was scarcely ever entrusted to a subject. In the middle ages, when the civil and military institutions were framed after the Chinese model, the Six Guards were founded, the Right and Left Horse Bureaux established, and other organizations, such as that of the Coast Guards, created.

The military system was thus completed, but, habituated to a prolonged state of peace, the Imperial Court gradually lost its administrative vigour; in course of time soldiers and farmers became distinct classes, and the early conscription system was replaced by an organization of volunteers, which finally produced the military class. The military power passed over entirely to the leaders of this class; through disturbances in the Empire the political power also fell into their hands; and for about seven centuries the military families held sway. Although these results followed from changes in the state of society and were beyond human control, they were deeply to be deplored, since they were contrary to the fundamental character of Our Empire and to the law of Our Imperial Ancestors.

Later on, in the eras of Kokwa and Kaéi, the decline of the Tokugawa Shogunate and the new aspect of foreign relations even threatened to impair our national dignity, causing no small anxiety to Our August Grandfather, the Emperor Ninko, and Our August Father, the Emperor Koméi, a fact which We recall with awe and gratitude. When in youth We succeeded to the Imperial Throne, the Shogun returned into Our hands the administrative power, and all the feudal lords their fiefs; thus, in a few years, Our entire realm was unified and the ancient régime restored. Due as this was to the meritorious services of Our loyal officers and wise councillors, civil and military, and to the abiding influence of Our Ancestors' benevolence towards the people, yet it must also be attributed to Our subjects' true sense of loyalty and their conviction of the importance of "Great Righteousness."

In consideration of these things, being desirous of reconstructing Our military system and of enhancing the glory of Our Empire, We have in the course of the last fifteen years established the present system of the Army and Navy. The supreme command of Our forces is in Our hands, and although We may entrust subordinate commands to Our subjects, yet the ultimate authority We Ourself shall hold and never delegate to any subject. It is Our will that this principle be carefully handed down to posterity and that the Emperor always retain the supreme civil and military power, so that the disgrace of the middle and succeeding ages may never be repeated. Soldiers and Sailors, We are your supreme Commander-in-Chief. Our relations with you will be most intimate when We rely upon you as Our limbs and you look up to Us as your head.

Whether We are able to guard the Empire, and so prove Ourself worthy of Heaven's blessings and repay the benevolence of Our Ancestors, depends upon the faithful discharge of your duties as soldiers and sailors. If the majesty and power of Our Empire be impaired, do you share with Us the sorrow; if the glory of Our arms shine resplendent, We will share with you the honour. If you all do your duty, and being one with Us in spirit do your utmost for the protection of the state, Our people will long enjoy the blessings of peace, and the might and dignity of our Empire will shine in the world. As We thus expect much of you, Soldiers and Sailors, We give you the following precepts:—

(1) The soldier and sailor should consider loyalty their essential duty. Who that is born in this land can be wanting in the spirit of grateful service to it? No soldier or sailor, especially, can be considered efficient unless this spirit be strong within him. A soldier or a sailor in whom the spirit is not strong, however skilled in art or proficient in science, is a mere puppet; and a body of soldiers or sailors wanting in loyalty, however well ordered and disciplined it may be, is in an emergency no better than a rabble. Remember that, as the protection of the state and the maintenance of its power depend upon the strength of its arms, the growth or decline of this strength must affect the nation's destiny for good or for evil; therefore neither be led astray by current opinions nor meddle in politics, but with single heart fulfil your essential duty of loyalty, and bear in mind that duty is weightier than a mountain, while death is lighter than a feather. Never by failing in moral principle fall into disgrace and bring dishonour upon your name.

(2) The soldier and the sailor should be strict in observing propriety. Soldiers and sailors are organized in grades, from the Marshal and the Admiral of the Fleet down to the private soldier or ordinary seaman; and even within the same rank and grade there are differences in seniority of service according to which juniors should submit to their seniors. Inferiors should regard the orders of their superiors as issuing directly from Us. Always pay due respect not only to your superiors but also to your seniors, even though not serving under them. On the other hand, superiors should never treat their inferiors with contempt or arrogance. Except when official duty requires them to be strict and severe, superiors should treat their inferiors with consideration, making kindness their chief aim, so that all grades may unite in their

service to the Emperor. If you, Soldiers and Sailors, neglect to observe propriety, treating your superiors with disrespect and your inferiors with harshness, and thus cause harmonious co-operation to be lost, you will not only be a blight upon the forces but also be unpardonable offenders against the state.

(3) The soldier and the sailor should esteem valour. Ever since the ancient times valour has in our country been held in high esteem, and without it Our subjects would be unworthy of their name. How then may the soldier and the sailor, whose profession it is to confront the enemy in battle, forget even for one instant to be valiant? But there is true valour and false. To be incited by mere impetuosity to violent action cannot be called true valour. The soldier and the sailor should have sound discrimination of right and wrong, cultivate self-possession, and form their plans with deliberation. Never to despise an inferior enemy or fear a superior, but to do one's duty as soldier or sailor—this is true valour. Those who thus appreciate true valour should in their daily intercourse set gentleness first and aim to win the love and esteem of others. If you affect valour and act with violence, the world will in the end detest you and look upon you as wild beasts. Of this you should take heed.

(4) The soldier and the sailor should highly value faithfulness and righteousness. Faithfulness and righteousness are the ordinary duties of man, but the soldier and the sailor, in particular, cannot be without them and remain in the ranks even for a day. Faithfulness implies the keeping of one's word and righteousness the fulfilment of one's duty. If then you wish to be faithful and righteous in any thing, you must carefully consider at the outset whether you can accomplish it or not. If you thoughtlessly agree to do something that is vague in its nature and bind yourself to unwise obligations, and then try to prove yourself faithful and righteous, you may find yourself in great straits from which there is no escape. In such cases your regrets will be of no avail. Hence you must first make sure whether the thing is righteous and reasonable or not. If you are convinced that you cannot possibly keep your word and maintain righteousness, you had better abandon your engagement at once. Ever since the

ancient times there have been repeated instances of great men and heroes who, overwhelmed by misfortune, have perished and left a tarnished name to posterity, simply because in their effort to be faithful in small matters they failed to discern right and wrong with reference to fundamental principles, or because, losing sight of the true path of public duty, they kept faith in private relations. You should, then, take serious warning by these examples.

(5) The soldier and the sailor should make simplicity their aim. If you do not make simplicity your aim, you will become effeminate and frivolous and acquire fondness for luxurious and extravagant ways; you will finally grow selfish and sordid and sink to the last degree of baseness, so that neither loyalty nor valour will avail to save you from the contempt of the world. It is not too much to say that you will thus fall into a life-long misfortune. If such an evil once makes its appearance among soldiers and sailors, it will certainly spread like an epidemic, and martial spirit and morale will instantly decline. Although, being greatly concerned on this point, We lately issued the Disciplinary Regulations and warned you against this evil, nevertheless, being harassed with anxiety lest it should break out, We hereby reiterate Our warning. Never do you, Soldiers and Sailors, make light of this injunction.

These five articles should not be disregarded even for a moment by soldiers and sailors. Now for putting them into practice, the all important is sincerity. These five articles are the soul of Our soldiers and sailors, and sincerity is the soul of these articles. If the heart be not sincere, words and deeds, however good, are all mere outward show and can avail nothing. If only the heart be sincere, anything can be accomplished. Moreover, these five articles are the Grand Way of Heaven and Earth and the universal law of humanity, easy to observe and to practice. If you, Soldiers and Sailors, in obedience to Our instruction, will observe and practice these principles and fulfil your duty of grateful service to the country, it will be a source of joy, not to Ourself alone, but to all people of Japan.

The 4th day of the 1st month of the 15th Year of Meiji.

— Reading No. 6 —

EDUCATIONAL RESCRIPT, 1890[6]

This rescript, issued on October 30, 1890, represents a reassertion of the nation's Confucian and Shinto ethics against Western political and moral ideas. It is also an attempt to utilize the traditional Japanese morality to support the new State which the Meiji oligarchs had just brought into being. It was frequently read in the schools and every Japanese was familiar with its contents.

"Know ye, Our Subjects!

"Our Imperial Ancestors have founded Our Empire on a basis broad and everlasting and have deeply and firmly implanted virtue; Our subjects, ever united in loyalty and filial piety, have from generation to generation illustrated the beauty thereof. This is the glory of the fundamental character of Our Empire, and herein also lies the source of Our education. Ye, Our subjects, be filial to your parents, affectionate to your brothers and sisters; as husbands and wives be harmonious, as friends true; bear yourselves in modesty and moderation; extend your benevolence to all; pursue learning and cultivate arts, and thereby develop your intellectual faculties and perfect your moral powers; furthermore, advance the public good and promote common interests; always respect the Constitution and observe the laws; should any emergency arise, offer yourselves courageously to the State; and thus guard and maintain the prosperity of Our Imperial Throne, coeval with heaven and earth. So shall ye not only be Our good and faithful subjects, but render illustrious the best traditions of your forefathers.

"The way here set forth is indeed the teaching bequeathed by Our Imperial Ancestors, to be observed alike by Their Descendants and subjects, infallible for all ages

[6] *The Japan Year Book 1939-1940* (Tokyo, 1939), p. 633.

and true in all places. It is Our wish to lay it to heart in all reverence, in common with you, Our subjects, that we may all thus attain to the same virtue."

The 30th day of the 10th month of the 23rd year Meiji.

— Reading No. 7 —

THE MEIJI CONSTITUTION[7]

Japanese liberals were disappointed with the conservative provisions of the Constitution, but they could not openly criticize it since it was presented as a gift from the Emperor. To make sure that no adverse remarks were publicized at the time of the promulgation, the Government suppressed all the radical journals and warned the rest not to comment unfavorably. Following is the complete text of the Meiji Constitution.

Preamble

Having, by virtue of the glories of Our Ancestors, ascended the Throne of a lineal succession unbroken for ages eternal; desiring to promote the welfare of, and to give development to the moral and intellectual faculties of Our beloved subjects, the very same that have been favored with the benevolent care and affectionate vigilance of Our Ancestors; and hoping to maintain the prosperity of the State, in concert with Our people and with their support, We hereby promulgate, in pursuance of Our Imperial Rescript of the 12th day of the 10th month of the 14th year of Meiji, a fundamental law of State, to exhibit the principles, by which We are to be guided in

---

[7] Text as in Ito Hirobumi, *Commentaries on the Constitution of the Empire of Japan,* translated by Ito Myoji (Tokyo, 1889), *passim.*

Our conduct, and to point out to what Our descendants and Our subjects and their descendants are forever to conform.

The rights of sovereignty of the State, We have inherited from Our Ancestors, and We shall bequeath them to Our descendants. Neither We nor they shall in future fail to wield them, in accordance with the provisions of the Constitution hereby granted.

We now declare to respect and protect the security of the rights and of the property of Our people, and to secure to them the complete enjoyment of the same, within the extent of the provisions of the present Constitution and of the law.

The Imperial Diet shall first be convoked for the 23rd year of Meiji and the time of its opening shall be the date when the present Constitution comes into force.

When in the future it may become necessary to amend any of the provisions of the present Constitution, We or Our successors shall assume the initiative right, and submit a project for the same to the Imperial Diet. The Imperial Diet shall pass its vote upon it, according to the conditions imposed by the present Constitution, and in no otherwise shall Our descendants or Our subjects be permitted to attempt any alteration thereof.

Our Ministers of State, on Our behalf, shall be held responsible for the carrying out of the present Constitution, and Our present and future subjects shall forever assume the duty of allegiance to the present Constitution.

Chapter I

The Emperor

ARTICLE I. The Empire of Japan shall be reigned over and governed by a line of Emperors unbroken for ages eternal.

ARTICLE II. The Imperial Throne shall be succeeded to by Imperial male descendants, according to the provisions of the Imperial House Law.

ARTICLE III. The Emperor is sacred and inviolable.

ARTICLE IV. The Emperor is the head of the Empire, combining in Himself the rights of sovereignty, and exercises them, according to the provisions of the present Constitution.

ARTICLE V. The Emperor exercises the legislative power with the consent of the Imperial Diet.

ARTICLE VI. The Emperor gives sanction to laws and orders them to be promulgated and executed.

ARTICLE VII. The Emperor convokes the Imperial Diet, opens, closes and prorogues it, and dissolves the House of Representatives.

ARTICLE VIII. The Emperor, in consequence of an urgent necessity to maintain public safety or to avert public calamities, issues, when the Imperial Diet is not sitting, Imperial Ordinances in the place of law.

Such Imperial Ordinances are to be laid before the Imperial Diet at its next session, and when the Diet does not approve the said Ordinances, the Government shall declare them to be invalid for the future.

ARTICLE IX. The Emperor issues or causes to be issued, the Ordinances necessary for the carrying out of the laws, or for the maintenance of the public peace and order, and for the promotion of the welfare of the subjects. But no Ordinance shall in any way alter any of the existing laws.

ARTICLE X. The Emperor determines the organization of the different branches of the administration, and salaries of all civil and military officers, and appoints and dismisses the same. Exceptions especially provided for in the present Constitution or in other laws, shall be in accordance with the respective provisions (bearing thereon).

ARTICLE XI. The Emperor has the supreme command of the Army and Navy.

ARTICLE XII. The Emperor determines the organization and peace standing of the Army and Navy.

ARTICLE XIII. The Emperor declares war, makes peace, and concludes treaties.

ARTICLE XIV. The Emperor declares a state of siege. The conditions and effects of a state of siege shall be determined by law.

ARTICLE XV. The Emperor confers titles of nobility, rank, orders and other marks of honor.

ARTICLE XVI. The Emperor orders amnesty, pardon, commutation of punishments and rehabilitation.

ARTICLE XVII. A Regency shall be instituted in conformity with the provisions of the Imperial House Law.

The Regent shall exercise the powers appertaining to the Emperor in His name.

Chapter II

Rights and Duties of Subjects

ARTICLE XVIII. The conditions necessary for being a Japanese subject shall be determined by law.

ARTICLE XIX. Japanese subjects may, according to qualifications determined in laws or ordinances, be appointed to civil or military or any other public offices equally.

ARTICLE XX. Japanese subjects are amenable to service in the Army or Navy, according to the provisions of law.

ARTICLE XXI. Japanese subjects are amenable to the duty of paying taxes, according to the provisions of law.

ARTICLE XXII. Japanese subjects shall have the liberty of abode and of changing the same within the limits of law.

ARTICLE XXIII. No Japanese subject shall be arrested, detained, tried or punished, unless according to law.

ARTICLE XXIV. No Japanese subject shall be deprived of his right of being tried by the judges determined by law.

ARTICLE XXV. Except in the cases provided for in the law, the house of no Japanese subject shall be entered or searched without his consent.

ARTICLE XXVI. Except in the cases mentioned in the law, the secrecy of the letters of every Japanese subject shall remain inviolate.

ARTICLE XXVII. The right of property of every Japanese subject shall remain inviolate.

Measures necessary to be taken for the public benefit shall be provided for by law.

ARTICLE XXVIII. Japanese subjects shall, within limits not prejudicial to peace and order, and not antagonistic to their duties as subjects, enjoy freedom of religious belief.

ARTICLE XXIX. Japanese subjects shall, within the limits of law, enjoy the liberty of speech, writing, publication, public meetings and associations.

ARTICLE XXX. Japanese subjects may present petitions,

by observing the proper forms of respect, and by complying with the rules specially provided for the same.

ARTICLE XXXI. The provisions contained in the present Chapter shall not affect the exercise of the powers appertaining to the Emperor, in times of war or in cases of a national emergency.

ARTICLE XXXII. Each and every one of the provisions contained in the preceding Articles of the present Chapter, that are not in conflict with the laws or the rules and discipline of the Army and Navy, shall apply to the officers and men of the Army and of the Navy.

Chapter III

The Imperial Diet

ARTICLE XXXIII. The Imperial Diet shall consist of two Houses, a House of Peers and a House of Representatives.

ARTICLE XXXIV. The House of Peers shall, in accordance with the Ordinance concerning the House of Peers, be composed of the members of the Imperial Family, of the orders of nobility, and of those persons who have been nominated thereto by the Emperor.

ARTICLE XXXV. The House of Representatives shall be composed of Members elected by the people, according to the provisions of the Law of Election.

ARTICLE XXXVI. No one can at one and the same time be a Member of both Houses.

ARTICLE XXXVII. Every law requires the consent of the Imperial Diet.

ARTICLE XXXVIII. Both Houses shall vote upon projects of law submitted to it by the Government, and may respectively initiate projects of law.

ARTICLE XXXIX. A bill, which has been rejected by either the one or the other of the two Houses, shall not be again brought in during the same session.

ARTICLE XL. Both Houses can make representations to the Government, as to laws or upon any other subject. When, however, such representations are not accepted, they cannot be made a second time during the same session.

ARTICLE XLI. The Imperial Diet shall be convoked every year.

ARTICLE XLII. A session of the Imperial Diet shall last during three months. In case of necessity, the duration of a session may be prolonged by Imperial Order.

ARTICLE XLIII. When urgent necessity arises, an extraordinary session may be convoked, in addition to the ordinary one.

The duration of an extraordinary session shall be determined by Imperial Order.

ARTICLE XLIV. The opening, closing, prolongation of session and prorogation of the Imperial Diet, shall be effected simultaneously for both Houses.

In case the House of Representatives has been ordered to dissolve, the House of Peers shall at the same time be prorogued.

ARTICLE XLV. When the House of Representatives has been ordered to dissolve, Members shall be caused by Imperial Order to be newly elected, and the new House shall be convoked within five months from the day of dissolution.

ARTICLE XLVI. No debate can be opened and no vote can be taken in either House of the Imperial Diet, unless not less than one third of the whole number of the Members thereof is present.

ARTICLE XLVII. Votes shall be taken in both Houses by absolute majority. In the case of a tie vote, the President shall have the casting vote.

ARTICLE XLVIII. The deliberations of both Houses shall be held in public. The deliberations may, however, upon demand of the Government or by resolution of the House, be held in secret sitting.

ARTICLE XLIX. Both Houses of the Imperial Diet may respectively present addresses to the Emperor.

ARTICLE L. Both Houses may receive petitions presented by subjects.

ARTICLE LI. Both Houses may enact, besides what is provided for in the present Constitution and in the Law of the Houses, rules necessary for the management of their internal affairs.

ARTICLE LII. No Member of either House shall be held responsible outside the respective Houses, for any opinion uttered or for any vote given in the House. When, however, a Member himself has given publicity to his opinions by public speech, by documents in print or in writing, or by any other similar means, he shall, in the matter, be amenable to the general law.

ARTICLE LIII. The Members of both Houses shall, during the session, be free from arrest, unless with the consent of the House, except in cases of flagrant delicts, or of offences connected with a state of internal commotion or with a foreign trouble.

ARTICLE LIV. The Ministers of State and the Delegates of the Government may, at any time, take seats and speak in either House.

Chapter IV

The Ministers of State and the Privy Council

ARTICLE LV. The respective Ministers of State shall give their advice to the Emperor, and be responsible for it.

All Laws, Imperial Ordinances and Imperial Rescripts of whatever kind, that relate to the affairs of the State, require the countersignature of a Minister of State.

ARTICLE LVI. The Privy Councillors shall, in accordance with the provisions for the organization of the Privy Council, deliberate upon important matters of State, when they have been consulted by the Emperor.

Chapter V

The Judicature

ARTICLE LVII. The Judicature shall be exercised by the Courts of Law according to law, in the name of the Emperor.

The organization of the Courts of Law shall be determined by law.

ARTICLE LVIII. The judges shall be appointed from among those who possess proper qualifications according to law.

No judge shall be deprived of his position, unless by way of criminal sentence or disciplinary punishment.

Rules for disciplinary punishment shall be determined by law.

ARTICLE LIX. Trials and judgments of a Court shall be conducted publicly. When, however, there exists any fear that such publicity may be prejudicial to peace and order, or to the maintenance of public morality, the public trial may be suspended by provision of law or by the decision of the Court of Law.

ARTICLE LX. All matters that fall within the competency of a special Court shall be specially provided for by law.

ARTICLE LXI. No suit at law, which relates to rights alleged to have been infringed by the illegal measures of the administrative authorities and which shall come within the competency of the Court of Administrative Litigation specially established by law, shall be taken cognizance of by a Court of Law.

Chapter VI

Finance

ARTICLE LXII. The imposition of a new tax or the modification of the rates (of an existing one) shall be determined by law.

However, all such administrative fees or other revenue having the nature of compensation shall not fall within the category of the above clause.

The raising of national loans and the contracting of other liabilities to the charge of the National Treasury, except those that are provided in the Budget, shall require the consent of the Imperial Diet.

ARTICLE LXIII. The taxes levied at present shall, in so far as they are not remodelled by a new law, be collected according to the old system.

ARTICLE LXIV. The expenditure and revenue of the State require the consent of the Imperial Diet by means of an annual Budget.

Any and all expenditures overpassing the appropriations set forth in the Titles and Paragraphs of the Budget, or that are not provided for in the Budget, shall subsequently require the approbation of the Imperial Diet.

ARTICLE LXV. The Budget shall be first laid before the House of Representatives.

ARTICLE LXVI. The expenditures of the Imperial House shall be defrayed every year out of the National Treasury, according to the present fixed amount for the same, and shall not require the consent thereto of the Imperial Diet, except in case an increase thereof is found necessary.

ARTICLE LXVII. Those already fixed expenditures based by the Constitution upon the powers appertaining to the Emperor, and such expenditures as may have arisen by the effect of law, or that appertain to the legal obligations of the Government, shall be neither rejected nor reduced by the Imperial Diet, without the concurrence of the Government.

ARTICLE LXVIII. In order to meet special requirements, the Government may ask the consent of the Imperial Diet to a certain amount as a Continuing Expenditure Fund, for a previously fixed number of years.

ARTICLE LXIX. In order to supply deficiencies, which are unavoidable, in the Budget, and to meet requirements unprovided for in the same, a Reserve Fund shall be provided in the Budget.

ARTICLE LXX. When the Imperial Diet cannot be convoked, owing to the external or internal condition of the country, in case of urgent need for the maintenance of public safety, the Government may take all necessary financial measures, by means of an Imperial Ordinance.

In the case mentioned in the preceding clause, the matter shall be submitted to the Imperial Diet at its next session, and its approbation shall be obtained thereto.

ARTICLE LXXI. When the Imperial Diet has not voted on the Budget, or when the Budget has not been brought into actual existence, the Government shall carry out the Budget of the preceding year.

ARTICLE LXXII. The final account of the expenditures and revenue of the State shall be verified and confirmed by the Board of Audit, and it shall be submitted by the Government to the Imperial Diet, together with the report of verification of the said Board.

The organization and competency of the Board of Audit shall be determined by law separately.

Chapter VII

Supplementary Rules

ARTICLE LXXIII. When it has become necessary in future to amend the provisions of the present Constitution, a project to the effect shall be submitted to the Imperial Diet by Imperial Order.

In the above case, neither House can open the debate, unless not less than two-thirds of the whole number of Members are present, and no amendment can be passed, unless a majority of not less than two-thirds of the Members present is obtained.

ARTICLE LXXIV. No modification of the Imperial House Law shall be required to be submitted to the deliberation of the Imperial Diet.

No provision of the present Constitution can be modified by the Imperial House Law.

ARTICLE LXXV. No modification can be introduced into the Constitution, or into the Imperial House Law, during the time of a Regency.

ARTICLE LXXVI. Existing legal enactments, such as laws, regulations, Ordinances, or by whatever names they may be called, shall, so far as they do not conflict with the present Constitution, continue in force.

All existing contracts or orders, that entail obligations upon the Government, and that are connected with expenditure, shall come within the scope of ARTICLE LXVII.

— Reading No. 8 —

THE TWENTY-ONE DEMANDS, 1915 [8]

Though the Japanese Government attempted to keep its negotiations with the Chinese secret, by February 1, 1915, U.S. Minister Paul Reinsch was able to send the

[8] *Foreign Relations of the United States: 1915* (Washington, 1924), pp. 99-103.

Department of State a fairly accurate summary of the demands. On March 6, 1915, he forwarded a copy of the original note along with the translation reproduced below.

I

The Japanese Government and the Chinese Government being desirous of maintaining the general peace in Eastern Asia and further strengthening the friendly relations and good neighborhood existing between the two nations, agree to the following articles:

ARTICLE I. The Chinese Government engages to give full assent to all matters upon which the Japanese Government may hereafter agree with the German Government relating to the disposition of all rights, interests and concessions which, by virtue of treaties or otherwise, Germany possesses in relation to the Province of Shantung.

ARTICLE II. The Chinese Government engages that within the Province of Shantung and along its coast no territory or island will be ceded or leased to a third power under any pretext.

ARTICLE III. The Chinese Government consents to Japan's building a railway from Chefoo or Lungkou to join the Kiaochou-Chinanfu Railway.

ARTICLE IV. The Chinese Government engages, in the interest of trade and for the residence of foreigners, to open by herself as soon as possible certain important cities and towns in the Province of Shantung as commercial ports. What places shall be opened are to be jointly decided upon by the two Governments in a separate agreement.

II

The Japanese Government and the Chinese Government, since the Chinese Government has always acknowledged the special position enjoyed by Japan in South Manchuria and Eastern Inner Mongolia, agree to the following articles:

ARTICLE I. The two contracting parties mutually agree that the term of lease of Port Arthur and Dalny and the term of lease of the South Manchurian Railway and the Antung-Mukden Railway shall be extended to the period of 99 years.

ARTICLE II. Japanese subjects (literally, Japanese officials or common people) in South Manchuria and Eastern Inner Mongolia shall have the right to lease or own land required either for erecting suitable buildings for trade and manufacture or for farming.

ARTICLE III. Japanese subjects (literally, Japanese officials or common people) shall be free to reside and travel in South Manchuria and Eastern Inner Mongolia and to engage in business and in manufacture of any kind whatsoever.

ARTICLE IV. The Chinese Government agrees to grant to Japanese subjects (literally, Japanese officials or common people) the mining rights of all the mines in South Manchuria and Eastern Inner Mongolia. As regards what mines are to be opened they shall be decided upon by the two Governments jointly. [*As regards the opening of each mine there shall be a separate agreement.—C.D.T.*]

ARTICLE V. The Chinese Government agrees that, in respect of the (two) cases mentioned herein below, the Japanese Government's consent shall be first obtained before action is taken:

(a) Whenever permission is granted to the subject of a third Power to build a railway or to make a loan with a third Power for the purpose of building a railway in South Manchuria and Eastern Inner Mongolia.

(b) Whenever a loan is to be made with a third Power pledging the local taxes of South Manchuria and Eastern Inner Mongolia as security.

ARTICLE VI. The Chinese Government agrees that if the Chinese Government employs political, financial or military advisers or instructors in South Manchuria or Eastern Inner Mongolia, the Japanese Government shall first be consulted.

ARTICLE VII. The Chinese Government agrees that the control and management of the Kirin-Changchun Railway shall be handed over to the Japanese Government for a term of 99 years dating from the signing of this agreement.

III

The Japanese Government and the Chinese Government, seeing that Japanese financiers and the Han-yeh-ping Company have close relations with each other at present and desiring that common interests of the two nations shall be advanced, agree to the following articles:

ARTICLE I. The two contracting parties mutually agree that when the opportune moment arrives the Han-yeh-ping Company shall be made a joint concern of the two nations; and they further agree that, without the previous consent of Japan, China shall not by her own act dispose of the rights and property of whatsoever nature of the said company nor cause the said company to dispose freely of the same.

ARTICLE II. The Chinese Government agrees that all mines in the neighborhood of those owned by the Han-yeh-ping Company shall not be permitted, without the consent of the said company, to be worked by other persons outside of the said company; and further agrees that if it is desired to carry out any undertaking which it is apprehended may directly or indirectly affect the interests of the said company, the consent of the said company shall first be obtained.

IV

The Japanese Government and the Chinese Government, with the object of effectively preserving the territorial integrity of China, agree to the following special article:

The Chinese Government engages not to cede or lease to a third Power any harbor or bay or island along the coast of China.

V

ARTICLE I. The Chinese Central Government shall employ influential Japanese (literally, Japanese who have strength, power, or influence) as advisers in political, financial and military affairs.

ARTICLE II. Japanese hospitals, churches and schools in the interior of China shall be granted the right of owning land.

ARTICLE III. Inasmuch as the Japanese Government and the Chinese Government have had many cases of dispute between Japanese and Chinese police to settle, cases which caused no little misunderstanding, it is for this reason necessary that the police departments of the important places (in China) shall be jointly administered by Japanese and Chinese or that the police departments of these places shall employ numerous Japanese, so that they may at the same time help to plan for the improvement of the Chinese police service.

ARTICLE IV. China shall purchase from Japan a fixed amount of munitions of war (say 50 percent or more of what is needed by the Chinese Government) or that there shall be established in China a Sino-Japanese jointly worked arsenal. Japanese technic-experts are to be employed and Japanese material to be purchased.

ARTICLE V. China agrees to grant to Japan with the right of constructing a railway connecting Wuchang with Kiukiang and Nanchang, another line between Nanchang and Hanchou, and another between Nanchang and Chaochou.

ARTICLE VI. If China needs foreign capital to work mines, build railways and construct harbor-works (including dock-yards) in the Province of Fukien, Japan shall be first consulted.

ARTICLE VII. China agrees that Japanese subjects shall have the right to propagate Buddhism (in Chinese text, reference is to religion and not especially to Buddhism) in China.

— Reading No. 9 —

THE TANAKA MEMORIAL, 1927[9]

Between June 27, and July 7, 1927, an important conference on Far Eastern affairs was held in Tokyo by Prime Minister Tanaka. It was attended by all the im-

[9] *The China Critic* (Shanghai), Vol. IV (1931), pp. 923-924.

*portant military and civil officials who had an interest in
this topic. The Tanaka Memorial, which was first published in 1929 by the Chinese, is supposed to be the
summary of the conclusions of this conference given by
Tanaka to the Emperor. It is highly doubtful if such a
document was ever presented to the Emperor. It may
well represent a working paper submitted by some member of the conference, or, and this is more likely, it may
be a very clever forgery. It has, however, a certain historical value, for it sums up a number of opinions which
were current in Japan in the late 1920's and which were
to dominate in the 1930's.*

Since the European War, Japan's political as well as
economic interests have been in an unsettled condition.
This is due to the fact that we have failed to take advantage of our special privileges in Manchuria and
Mongolia and fully to realize our acquired rights. But
upon my appointment as premier, I was instructed to
guard our interests in this region and watch for opportunities for further expansion. Such injunctions one
cannot take lightly. Ever since I advocated a positive
policy towards Manchuria and Mongolia as a common
citizen, I have longed for its realization. So in order that
we may lay plans for the colonization of the Far East
and the development of our new continental empire, a
special conference was held from June 27th to July 7th
lasting in all eleven days. It was attended by all the civil
and military officers connected with Manchuria and
Mongolia, whose discussions resulted in the following resolutions. These we respectfully submit to Your Majesty
for consideration.

General Considerations

The term Manchuria and Mongolia includes the provinces Fengtien, Kirin, Heilungkiang and Outer and Inner
Mongolia. It extends an area of 74,000 square miles,
having a population of 28,000,000 people. The territory
is more than three times as large as our own empire not
counting Korea and Formosa, but it is inhabited by only
one-third as many people. The attractiveness of the land
does not arise from the scarcity of population alone; its

wealth of forestry, minerals and agricultural products is also unrivalled elsewhere in the world. In order to exploit these resources for the perpetuation of our national glory, we created especially the South Manchuria Railway Company. The total investment involved in our undertakings in railway, shipping, mining, forestry, steel, manufacture, agriculture, and in cattle raising, as schemes pretending to be mutually beneficial to China and Japan, amount to no less than Yen 440,000,000. It is veritably the largest single investment and the strongest organization of our country. Although nominally the enterprise is under the joint ownership of the government and the people, in reality the government has complete power and authority. In so far as the South Manchuria Railway is empowered to undertake diplomatic, police, and ordinary administrative functions so that it may carry out our imperialistic policies, the Company forms a peculiar organization which has exactly the same powers as the Governor-General of Korea. This fact alone is sufficient to indicate the immense interests we have in Manchuria and Mongolia. Consequently the policies towards this country of successive administrations since Meiji are all based on his injunctions, elaborating and continuously completing the development of the new continental empire in order to further the advance of our national glory and prosperity for countless generations to come.

Unfortunately, since the European War there have been constant changes in diplomatic as well as domestic affairs. The authorities of the Three Eastern Provinces [*Manchuria*] are also awakened and gradually work toward reconstruction and industrial development following our example. Their progress is astonishing. It has affected the spread of our influence in a most serious way, and has put us to so many disadvantages that the dealings with Manchuria and Mongolia of successive governments have resulted in failure. Furthermore, the restriction of the Nine-Power Treaty signed at the Washington Conference have reduced our special rights and privileges in Manchuria and Mongolia to such an extent that there is no freedom left for us. The very existence of our country is endangered. Unless these obstacles are removed, our national existence will be insecure and our national

strength will not develop. Moreover, the resources of
wealth are congregated in North Manchuria. If we do not
have the right of way here, it is obvious that we shall not
be able to tap the riches of this country. Even the resources of South Manchuria which we won by the Russo-
Japanese War will also be greatly restricted by the Nine-
Power Treaty. The result is that while our people cannot
migrate into Manchuria as they please, the Chinese are
flowing in as a flood. Hordes of them move into the
Three Eastern Provinces every year, numbering in the
neighborhood of several millions. They have jeopardized
our acquired rights in Manchuria and Mongolia to such
an extent that our annual surplus population of eight
hundred thousand has no place to seek refuge. In view of
this we have to admit our failure in trying to effect a
balance between our population and food supply. If we
do not devise plans to check the influx of Chinese im-
migrants immediately, in five years' time the number of
Chinese will exceed 6,000,000. Then we shall be confronted with greater difficulties in Manchuria and Mongolia.

It will be recalled that when the Nine-Power Treaty
was signed which restricted our movements in Manchuria
and Mongolia, public opinion was greatly aroused. The
late Emperor Taisho called a conference of Yamagata
and other high officers of the army and navy to find a
way to counteract this new engagement. I was sent to
Europe and America to ascertain secretly the attitude of
the important statesmen toward it. They were all agreed
that the Nine-Power Treaty was initiated by the United
States. The other Powers which signed it were willing to
see our influence increase in Manchuria and Mongolia
in order that we may protect the interests of international
trade and investments. This attitude I found out person-
ally from the political leaders of England, France and
Italy. The sincerity of these expressions could be depended upon. Unfortunately, just as we were ready to
carry out our policy and declare void the Nine-Power
Treaty with the approval of those whom I met on my
trip, the Seiyukai cabinet suddenly fell and our policy
failed of fruition. It was indeed a great pity. After I
had secretly exchanged views with the Powers regarding

the development of Manchuria and Mongolia, I returned by way of Shanghai. At the wharf there a Chinese attempted to take my life. An American woman was hurt, but I escaped by the divine protection of my emperors of the past. It seems that it was by divine will that I should assist Your Majesty to open a new era in the Far East and to develop the new continental empire.

The Three Eastern Provinces are politically the imperfect spot in the Far East. For the sake of self-protection as well as the protection of others, Japan cannot remove the difficulties in Eastern Asia unless she adopts the policy of "Blood and Iron." But in carrying out this policy we have to face the United States which has been turned against us by China's policy of fighting poison with poison. In the future if we want to control China, we must first crush the United States just as in the past we had to fight in the Russo-Japanese War. But in order to conquer China we must first conquer Manchuria and Mongolia. In order to conquer the world, we must first conquer China. If we succeed in conquering China the rest of the Asiatic countries and the South Sea Countries will fear us and surrender to us. Then the world will realize that Eastern Asia is ours and will not dare to violate our rights. This is the plan left to us by Emperor Meiji, the success of which is essential to our national existence.

The Nine-Power Treaty is entirely an expression of the spirit of commercial rivalry. It was the intention of England and America to crush our influence in China with their power of wealth. The proposed reduction of armaments is nothing but a means to limit our military strength, making it impossible for us to conquer the vast territory of China. On the other hand, China's sources of wealth will be entirely at their disposal. It is merely a scheme by which England and America may defeat our plans. And yet the Minseito made the Nine-Power Treaty the important thing and emphasized our TRADE rather than our RIGHTS in China. This is a mistaken policy— a policy of national suicide. England can afford to talk about trade relations only because she has India and Australia to supply her with foodstuffs and other materials. So can America because South America and Canada are there to supply her needs. Their spare energy could be entirely devoted to developing trade in China to enrich themselves.

But in Japan her food supply and raw materials decrease in proportion to her population. If we merely hope to develop trade, we shall eventually be defeated by England and America, who possess unsurpassable capitalistic power. In the end, we shall get nothing. A more dangerous factor is the fact that the people of China might some day wake up. Even during these years of internal strife, they can still toil patiently, and try to imitate and displace our goods so as to impair the development of our trade. When we remember that the Chinese are our sole customers, we must beware lest one day China becomes unified and her industries become prosperous. Americans and Europeans will compete with us; our trade in China will be wrecked. Minseito's proposal to uphold the Nine-Power Treaty and to adopt the policy of trade towards Manchuria is nothing less than a suicide policy.

After studying the present conditions and possibilities of our country, our best policy lies in the direction of taking positive steps to secure rights and privileges in Manchuria and Mongolia. These will enable us to develop our trade. This will not only forestall China's own industrial development, but also prevent the penetration of European Powers. This is the best policy possible!

The way to gain actual rights in Manchuria and Mongolia is to use this region as a base and under the pretence of trade and commerce penetrate the rest of China. Armed by the rights already secured we shall seize the resources all over the country. Having China's entire resources at our disposal we shall proceed to conquer India, the Archipelago, Asia Minor, Central Asia, and even Europe. But to get control of Manchuria and Mongolia is the first step if the Yamato race wishes to distingush itself on Continental Asia. Final success belongs to the country having raw materials; the full growth of national strength belongs to the country having extensive territory. If we pursue a positive policy to enlarge our rights in Manchuria and China, all these prerequisites of a powerful nation will constitute no problem. Furthermore our surplus population of 700,000 each year will also be taken care of.

If we want to inaugurate a new policy and secure the permanent prosperity of our empire, a positive policy towards Manchuria and Mongolia is the only way. . . .

— Reading No. 10 —

THE AMAU STATEMENT, 1934

The Amau Statement was occasioned by Japan's resentment of the increasing amount of aid which the Western Powers were giving to China. At Geneva the League of Nations had just received the Rjachman report on assistance to China. Curtiss-Wright had set up an airplane factory. The United States had sold fighter planes to the Chinese, and a retired American officer was supervising combat pilot training. In addition, a German general had just become chief military adviser in Nanking. Document A is the original statement made by Amau Eiji, a Foreign Ministry official, on April 17, 1934. As a result of foreign reaction, Hirota Koki, the Foreign Minister, issued a second statement toning down the first. (Document B.) It will be noted that even Hirota still asserted Japan's responsibility for law and order in East Asia.

A

Original Statement by Amau Eiji, April 17, 1934 [10]

Owing to the special position of Japan in her relations with China, her views and attitude respecting matters that concern China may not agree in every point with those of

[10] *Foreign Relations of the United States: Japan 1931-1941* (2 vols., Washington, 1943), I, 224.

foreign nations: but it must be realized that Japan is called upon to exert the utmost effort in carrying out her mission and in fulfilling her special responsibilities in East Asia.

Japan has been compelled to withdraw from the League of Nations because of their failure to agree in their opinions on the fundamental principles of preserving peace in East Asia. Although Japan's attitude toward China, may at times differ from that of foreign countries, such difference cannot be evaded, owing to Japan's position and mission.

It goes without saying that Japan at all times is endeavoring to maintain and promote her friendly relations with foreign nations, but at the same time we consider it only natural that, to keep peace and order in East Asia, we must even act alone on our own responsibility and it is our duty to perform it. At the same time, there is no country but China which is in a position to share with Japan the responsibility for the maintenance of peace in East Asia. Accordingly, unification of China, preservation of her territorial integrity, as well as restoration of order in that country, are most ardently desired by Japan. History shows that these can be attained through no other means than the awakening and the voluntary efforts of China herself. We oppose therefore any attempt on the part of China to avail herself of the influence of any other country in order to resist Japan: We also oppose any action taken by China, calculated to play one power against another. Any joint operations undertaken by foreign powers even in the name of technical or financial assistance at this particular moment after the Manchurian and Shanghai Incidents are bound to acquire political significance. Undertakings of such nature, if carried through to the end, must give rise to complications that might eventually necessitate discussion of problems like fixing spheres of influence or even international control or division of China, which would be the greatest possible misfortune for China and at the same time would have the most serious repercussion upon Japan and East Asia. Japan therefore must object to such undertakings as a matter of principle, although she will not find it necessary

to interfere with any foreign country negotiating indi-
vidually with China on questions of finance or trade, as
long as such negotiations benefit China and are not detrimental to the maintenance of peace in East Asia.

However, supplying China with war planes, building
aerodromes in China and detailing military instructors or
military advisers to China or contracting a loan to provide
funds for political uses, would obviously tend to alienate
the friendly relations between Japan and China and
other countries and to disturb peace and order in East
Asia. Japan will oppose such projects.

The foregoing attitude of Japan should be clear from
the policies she has pursued in the past. But, on account
of the fact that positive movements for joint action in
China by foreign powers under one pretext or another
are reported to be on foot, it is deemed not inappropriate
to reiterate her policy at this time.

B

Statement by Hirota Koki [11]

Japan has not infringed upon China's independence or
interests, nor has she the intention to do so. In fact, she
sincerely desires the preservation of territorial integrity of
China and her unification and prosperity. These ends
should, fundamentally speaking, be attained by China
herself through her self-awakening and voluntary efforts.

Japan has no intention to trespass upon the rights of
other powers in China. Their bona fide financial and
commercial activities will redound to the benefit of China
which is quite welcome to Japan. She, of course, sub-
scribes to the principles of the open door and equal
opportunity in China. She is observing scrupulously all
existing treaties and agreements concerning that country.

However, Japan cannot remain indifferent to anyone's
taking action under any pretext, which is prejudicial to the
maintenance of law and order in East Asia for which she,
if only in view of her geographic position, has the most

---

[11] *Foreign Relations of the United States: Diplomatic Papers
1934* (5 vols., Washington, 1950), III, 140-41.

vital concern. Consequently, she cannot afford to have questions of China exploited by any third party for the execution of a selfish policy which does not take into consideration the above circumstances.

— Reading No. 11 —

SUMMARY OF FUNDAMENTAL NATIONAL POLICY[12]

This policy announcement was made by the second Konoe cabinet on August 1, 1940. Basically, it called for an internal reorganization which would permit the nation to utilize its full potential strength in taking advantage of the opportunity created by the German victories in Europe for the establishment of the "new order in Greater East Asia."

The world stands at a great historic turning point, and it is about to witness the creation of new forms of government, economy, and culture, based upon the growth and development of sundry groups of states. Japan, too, is confronted by a great trial such as she has never experienced in history. In order to carry out fully at this juncture our national policy in accordance with the lofty spirit in which the country was founded, it is an important task of urgent necessity to us that we should grasp the inevitable trends in the developments of world history, effect speedily fundamental renovations along all lines of government, and strive for the perfection of a

[12] *Foreign Relations of the United States: Japan 1931-1941* (2 vols., Washington, 1943), II, 108-11.

state structure for national defense. Accordingly, the general lines of the country's fundamental national policies have been formulated as follows:

SUMMARY OF FUNDAMENTAL NATIONAL POLICIES

1. Basic Policy

The basic aim of Japan's national policy lies in the firm establishment of world peace in accordance with the lofty spirit of Hakko Ichiu, in which the country was founded, and in the construction, as the first step, of a new order in Greater East Asia, having for its foundation the solidarity of Japan, Manchoukuo and China.

Japan will, therefore, devote the total strength of the nation to the fulfilment of the above policy by setting up swiftly an unshakable national structure of her own adapted to meet the requirements of new developments both at home and abroad.

2. National Defense and Foreign Policy

The Government will strive for the repletion of armaments adequate for the execution of the national policies, by taking into consideration the new developments both at home and abroad, and constructing a state structure for national defense, capable of bringing into full play the total strength of the nation.

Japan's foreign policy, which aims ultimately at the construction of a new order in Greater East Asia, will be directed, first of all, toward a complete settlement of the China Affair, and the advancement of the national fortune by taking a far-sighted view of the drastic changes in the international situation and formulating both constructive and flexible measures.

3. Renovation of Internal Structure

What is urgently required in internal administration is the laying of the foundation for a state structure for national defense through a complete renovation of the domestic administration in general, for which purpose the Government expects the realization of the following points:

A. Renovation of education thoroughly in harmony with the fundamental principles of the national polity, and also the establishment of ethical principles of the nation stressing, above all, service to the state and eradicating all selfish and materialistic thoughts.

B. Establishment of a powerful new political structure and a unified control of government affairs.

a. Establishment of a new national structure, of which the keynote lies in the service to the state through the co-operation between government and people, every man according to his sphere of profession or business.

b. Renovation of the Diet as an organ for assisting the Throne, so as to adapt it to the new national structure.

c. Fundamental renovation in the operation of administrative organs, and the reformation of the bureaucracy, aimed at the unity and efficiency of those organs.

C. Laying the foundation of national defense economy, of which the keynote is to lie in the autonomous development of the economy of Japan, Manchoukuo and China with Japan as the center.

a. Establishment of a sphere of co-operative economies, with the Japan-Manchoukuo-China group as one of the units.

b. Inauguration of a planned economy through the co-operation between government and people, and especially the perfection of a unitary control system covering the production, distribution and consumption of important commodities.

c. Establishment of a financial scheme and reinforcement of banking control, directed toward the development of the nation's total economic power.

d. Renovation of the foreign trade policy so as to adapt it to the new world situation.

e. Establishment of the measures for self-sufficiency in the people's daily necessities especially in the principal foodstuffs.

f. An epoch-making expansion of the vital industries —especially heavy, chemical and machine industries.

g. An epoch-making promotion of science, and rationalization of production.

h. Perfection and extension of the communication

and transportation facilities so as to adapt them to the
new developments at home and abroad.

    i. Establishment of land development plans aiming
at the enhancement of the total national strength.

    j. Inauguration of permanent measures concerning
the promotion of the stamina and physical strength of
the nation, and especially the fundamental measures concerning the security and development of agriculture and
agricultural communities.

    k. Rectification of the inequality in individual sacri-
fices incident to the execution of national policies; full
operation of various welfare measures, and renovation of
the living mode of the nation, and the maintenance of
such standard of living as will enable the nation to lead a
plain, solid and vigorous life and to surmount the national
crisis by persevering truly through years of hardship.

— Reading No. 12 —

JAPAN DECIDES ON WAR

    The three items in this reading are all taken from the
Memoirs *of Prince Konoe. The first selection is the
agenda for the conference at which the Japanese leaders
decided to continue their policies even if it meant war.
The second selection clearly demonstrates the Emperor's
personal opposition to the war, an opposition which was
ineffective because his conception of his role as a constitutional monarch obliged him to accept the counsel of
his duly established advisers. The third selection nicely
summarizes the divisions of opinion among the military
and civil officials on the eve of war.*

A

IMPERIAL CONFERENCE, SEPTEMBER 6, 1941 [13]

*Plans for the Prosecution of the Policy of the Imperial
Government*
(*Agenda for a Council in the Imperial Presence*)

In view of the increasingly critical situation, especially
the aggressive plans being carried out by America,
England, Holland and other countries, the situation in
Soviet Russia and the Empire's latent potentialties, the
Japanese Government will proceed as follows in carrying
out its plans for the southern territories as laid in "An
Outline of the Policy of the Imperial Government in
View of Present Developments."

1. Determined not to be deterred by the possibility of
being involved in a war with America (and England and
Holland) in order to secure our national existence, we
will proceed with war preparations so that they be completed approximately toward the end of October.

2. At the same time, we will endeavor by every possible diplomatic means to have our demands agreed to by
America and England. Japan's minimum demands in
these negotiations with America (and England), together
with the Empire's maximum concessions, are embodied
in the attached document.

3. If by the early part of October there is no reasonable
hope of having our demands agreed to in the diplomatic
negotiations mentioned above, we will immediately make
up our minds to get ready for war against America (and
England and Holland).

Policies with reference to countries other than those in
the southern territories will be carried out in harmony
with the plans already laid. Special effort will be made to
prevent America and Soviet Russia from forming a united
front against Japan.

[13] The *Konoe Memoirs,* as reprinted in U.S. Congress, Joint
Committee on the Investigation of the Pearl Harbor Attack, *Hearings* (39 parts, Washington, 1946), part 20,
4022-23.

ANNEX DOCUMENT

A List of Japan's Minimum Demands and Her Maximum Concessions in Her Negotiations with America and England

I. Japan's Minimum Demands in Her Negotiations with America (and England).

1. America and England shall not intervene in or obstruct a settlement by Japan of the China Incident.

(a) They will not interfere with Japan's plan to settle the China Incident in harmony with the Sino-Japanese Basic Agreement [14] and the Japan-China-Manchoukuo Tripartite Declaration.

(b) America and England will close the Burma Route and offer the Chiang Regime neither military, political nor economic assistance.

Note: The above do not run counter to Japan's previous declarations in the "N" plan for the settlement of the China Incident. In particular, the plan embodied in the new Sino-Japanese Agreement for the stationing of Japanese troops in the specified areas will be rigidly adhered to. However, the withdrawal of troops other than those mentioned above may be guaranteed in principle upon the settlement of the China Incident.

Commercial operations in China on the part of America and England may also be guaranteed, in so far as they are purely commercial.

2. America and England will take no action in the Far East which offers a threat to the defense of the Empire.

(a) America and England will not establish military bases in Thai [land], the Netherlands East Indies, China or Far Eastern Soviet Russia.

(b) Their Far Eastern military forces will not be increased over their present strength.

Note: Any demands for the liquidation of Japan's special relations with French Indo-China based on the Japanese-French Agreement will not be considered.

[14] This refers to an agreement made with the puppet government at Peking.

3. America and England will cooperate with Japan in her attempt to obtain needed raw materials.

(a) America and England will restore trade relations with Japan and furnish her with the raw materials she needs from the British and American territories in the Southwest Pacific.

(b) America and England will assist Japan to establish close economic relations with Thai [land] and the Netherlands East Indies.

II. Maximum Concessions by Japan.

It is first understood that our minimum demands as listed under I above will be agreed to.

1. Japan will not use French Indo-China as a base for operations against any neighboring countries with the exception of China.

Note: In case any questions are asked concerning Japan's attitude towards Soviet Russia, the answer is to be that as long as Soviet Russia faithfully carries out the Neutrality Pact and does not violate the spirit of the agreement by, for instance, threatening Japan or Manchuria, Japan will not take any military action.

2. Japan is prepared to withdraw her troops from French Indo-China as soon as a just peace is established in the Far East.

3. Japan is prepared to guarantee the neutrality of the Philippine Islands.

B

An Imperial Query[15]

Thus it came about that on September 6th, at a conference held in the Imperial presence, the "Outline for the Execution of the National Policy of the Imperial Government" was decided upon.

On the day before the conference held in the Imperial presence, I had an audience with the Emperor in order to informally discuss the "Outline for the Execution of the National Policy of the Imperial Government." The Emperor, in examining the program, pointed out that it placed war preparations first and diplomatic negotiations

[15] The *Konoe Memoirs, op. cit.,* pp. 4004-05.

second. This, he said, would seem to give precedence to war over diplomatic activities. He expressed the desire to question the chiefs of the Army and Navy General Staffs regarding this point at the meeting on the following day. In reply I explained that the order of business in the program did not indicate any differences in degree of importance. I also said that the Government intended to pursue diplomatic negotiations as long as possible and to commence preparations for war only when there seemed no prospect of successful negotiations. I also suggested that if he wished to question the Chiefs of the Supreme Command on the subject, perhaps it would be more advisable to summon them privately rather than question them at the conference. The Emperor requested that they be summoned at once. They arrived promptly and in my presence were asked the same question and gave the same answer that I had given.

In continuing, the Emperor asked the Army Chief of Staff, General Sugiyama, what was the Army's belief as to the probable length of hostilities in case of a Japanese-American war. The Chief of Staff replied that he believed operations in the South Pacific could be disposed of in about three months. Turning to the Chief of Staff, the Emperor recalled that the General had been Minister of War at the time of the outbreak of the China Incident, and that he had then informed the Throne that the incident would be disposed of in about one month. He pointed out that, despite the General's assurance, the incident was not yet concluded after four long years of fighting. In trepidation the Chief of Staff went to great lengths to explain that the extensive hinterland of China prevented the consummation of operations according to the scheduled plan. At this the Emperor raised his voice and said that, if the Chinese hinterland was extensive, the Pacific was boundless. He asked how the General could be certain of his three month calculation. The Chief of Staff hung his head, unable to answer.

At this point the Navy Chief of General Staff lent a helping hand to Sugiyama by saying that to his mind Japan was like a patient suffering from a serious illness. He said the patient's case was so critical that the question of whether or not to operate had to be determined without delay. Should he be let alone without an operation, there was danger of a gradual decline. An operation, while it might be extremely dangerous, would still offer some hope of saving his life. The stage was now reached, he said, where a quick decision had to be made one way or the other. He felt that the Army General Staff was in favor of putting hope in diplomatic negotiations to the finish, but that in case of failure a decisive operation would have to be performed. To this extent, then, he was in favor of the negotiation proposals. The Emperor, pursuing the point, asked the Chiefs of the Supreme Command if it was not true that both of them were for giving precedence to diplomacy, and both answered in the affirmative.

The Conference was held on September 6th at 10 A.M. in the Imperial presence. During the conference the President of the Privy Council, Yoshimichi Hara, spoke up and said the proposal before the conference gave the impression that the emphasis was being placed upon war rather than upon diplomacy. He wished a clarification of the views of the Government and the Supreme Command on this point. The Navy Minister, representing the Government, answered Hara's question, but the Chiefs of the Supreme Command remained silent.

The Emperor now spoke up suddenly and seconded the opinion put forth by the President of the Privy Council, Hara, and expressed his regret that the Supreme Command had not seen fit to answer. He then took from his pocket a piece of paper on which was written a poem by the Emperor Meiji: "Since all are brothers in this world, why is there such constant turmoil?" After reading this poem aloud, the Emperor stressed that he had read it over and over again and that he was striving to introduce into the present the Emperor Meiji's ideal of international peace. Everyone present was struck with awe, and there was silence throughout the hall. Soon the Chief of the Navy General Staff, Admiral Nagano, rose and said that he was filled with trepidation at the prospect of the Emperor's displeasure with the Supreme Command. The truth was, he said, that when the Navy Minister spoke, he had been under the impression that the Navy Minister was representing both the Government and the Supreme Command, and he had therefore remained silent. He assured the Emperor that the Chiefs of the Supreme Command most certainly concurred with the Navy Minister's answer; that they too were conscious of the importance of diplomacy, and advocated a resort to armed force only when there seemed no other way out. The meeting adjourned in an atmosphere of unprecedented tenseness.

C

JAPANESE OPINION, LATE 1941 [16]

I. Differences between the Viewpoint of the Government and the Army.

1. Concerning the "Decisions Reached at the Council in the Imperial Presence: Clause 3 of the Plans for the Prosecution of the Imperial Program," as decided upon at the Council in the Imperial Presence on September 6th, states: "If by the early part of October, there is no reasonable hope to have our demands agreed to—we will immediately make up our minds to get ready for war against America, England and Holland." The Army takes the position that the progress of the negotiations with America in the early part of October impels us to decide that "there is no reasonable hope to have our demands agreed to," as referred to in the said article and that, therefore, the conclusion is inevitable that by the middle or end of October we "must make up our minds to ready for war."

The Cabinet contends that not only have the diplomatic negotiations not reached a hopeless state, but that in the light of the diplomatic documents which we have received from America and many other reports, the American Government also entertains considerable hope of arriving at a satisfactory agreement. However, that Government harbors certain misunderstandings and suspicion (for example, the Army's gradual infiltration into Northern Indo-China in the early part of October, though, of course, this was carried out in harmony with definite treaty stipulations); is influenced by the deliberate mis-

[16] *Ibid.*, pp. 4026-28.

representations of certain Third Powers, or is carefully watching the future of the international situation, especially of the European War. There are also activities on the part of strong anti-Japanese elements in the Far Eastern Sections of the State Department, activities which have covered up the true feelings of the President and Secretary of State Hull. In view of these facts, we can not decide that there is no hope of successful negotiations even with the present conditions as suggested by us, if time is allowed for the conduct of the negotiations. Especially, if we could get our Army authorities to relax their position somewhat, namely, with reference to the withdrawal of troops, we believe that there is a good possibility of reaching an agreement.

The Army feels that although the early part of October is the ideal time for us to decide on war in harmony with the demands of the Supreme Command, it can defer it till the middle of the month, but by all means not later than the latter part of the month. Otherwise, the Army feels itself seriously handicapped in the event of war. It, therefore, rigidly adheres to the middle of the month, the latter part of October, as the time to decide upon war, should war be decided upon, and this is a point that must ever be kept in mind.

2. The obstacles in the negotiations with America (especially the problem of the withdrawal of troops); Diplomatic negotiations are still proceeding with America and while the true intentions of that country are not clear the following three points may be listed as the major unsolved problems:

(1) The problem of stationing or withdrawal of troops from China.

(2) Japan's attitude toward the Tripartite Pact.

(3) The problem of non-discriminatory trade in the Pacific area.

Among the three, it is clear to all that the outstanding problem is the withdrawal of troops. In other words, that problem is really the one problem, the negotiations with America.

A summary of the Army's attitude concerning the withdrawal of troops is as follows:

Our Government's terms for a Sino-Japanese peace, as

indicated to America, are very liberal, inasmuch as they include the principles of no annexation and no reparations. They merely insist on the stationing of troops in certain areas for a stipulated period in order to facilitate cooperation with China in preventing the inroads of communism and any other movements tending to disrupt the present order. It is evident that these dangers are a threat to the safety of both Japan and China and to the welfare and prosperity of the peoples of both countries. These measures are also vitally necessary for the economic development of the country. It is, of course, understood that all troops not necessary for the above purposes will be withdrawn as soon as the China Incident is brought to a close. In view of the above, the stationing of troops in China is an absolutely necessary stipulation. In other words, the Army insists that this point is a consideration of first importance and that the stationing of these troops in China is, after all, the one and only tangible result of the China Incident. It follows that the Army can not agree to any plan which envisages the giving up of the right to station troops in China. If our troops' withdrawal from China is carried out, the Army will be overcome by a spirit of defeatism and it will be impossible to preserve its morale.

On the other hand, the final position of America on this matter of stationing troops is not yet clear. It may be possible if we give time for further negotiations to have our terms for the China problem agreed to by America. Up to the present, the American position in this matter seems to be as follows:

(1) Japan is to agree in principle to the withdrawal of troops. (The matter of stationing troops in China must be decided after this principle has been accepted.) It is not clear at the present moment whether America will agree to the stationing of troops in China but in the light of the negotiations so far conducted, America's position does not seem to be entirely negative in the matter.

(2) America desires to be assured of Japan's sincerity in the matter of the withdrawal of troops. For instance, Under-Secretary Welles stated to Minister Wakasugi in Washington that, if Japan was sincere in her decision

to withdraw the troops, America was willing to give
more consideration to the manner in which this should be
done.

In light of the above, the Cabinet's position in regard
to the withdrawal of troops is as follows:

(1) Diplomatic negotiations should be continued for
a longer period.

(2) We understand, of course, that the stationing of
troops in China is a very necessary consideration. However, if the success or failure of the present negotiations
hangs on this one problem, the Cabinet holds the view
that it would be better for us to agree to the American
formula for the withdrawal of troops and yet secure stationing of troops in China for a specified period.

3. Views in Regard to War Against America: the
Army points out that as a result of the British and American freezing orders, the import of necessary materials
(especially oil) has become almost impossible and our
shortages will become so severe that, should America
come upon us with impossible demands, we shall find
ourselves unable to resist even for the sake of defending
our very existence. Therefore, the Army insists that even
though the situation is fraught with certain dangers,
there is no cause for alarm and that now is the time for us
to take decisive action if our people stand united in a
determination to overcome all obstacles, remembering
that America as well as Japan has certain weaknesses.

The Army claims that if we propose too liberal terms
through American good offices and settle the China Incident, China would learn to despise Japan and we would
have to punish her again within two or three years.

I, as the Prime Minister, on the other hand, could not
possibly entertain the idea of plunging into a great war
with all its uncertainties at a time when the China Incident
is still unsettled. Although, as the result of the freezing,
we are faced with gradually shrinking stores of munitions
of war, we believe that it is possible to take other means
of replenishing our supplies, especially with reference to
oil. For even if we should capture the Netherlands East
Indies, the necessary amount of oil could not be obtained
within a year or two because installations would be
destroyed and transportation would be difficult. It would

be far better for us, instead of going to war, to mobilize all our labor and material resources and begin the manufacture of synthetic oil. We think it would not be impossible to produce 500,000 tons by the end of 1943 and 4,000,000 tons during 1944. As a result of our four years of struggle in China, our national strength has considerably deteriorated and the morale of our people has declined. Would it not be better at this time for us to eat the bitter [gall], preserve our as yet undamaged Navy, settle the China Incident, and gradually build up our national strength?

4. The Attitude of the Navy: The following is a summary of the Navy's attitude:

At the present time, we stand at the parting of the ways where we must make up our minds to either carry on diplomatic negotiations to the bitter end or declare war. If we decide to follow the path of diplomatic negotiations, we must make up our minds to give up the idea of declaring war. For us to carry on diplomatic negotiations for two or three months and then to declare war because we decide that further diplomatic negotiations would be fruitless is an impossibility. However, the question as to whether we are going to declare war or choose the plan of diplomatic negotiation is one which the Government must decide. In other words, the Prime Minister must make the decision as to whether we are going to turn to the left or to the right. There are some in Navy circles who hold that war should be avoided at all costs and that we should do our best to adjust our relations with America through diplomatic negotiations.

PRINCE KONOE'S RESIGNATION [17]

In this document Prince Konoe places the responsibility for the decision to make war squarely on Tojo Hideki, the chief spokesman for the Army.

At the time when I was honored for the third time with the totally unexpected Imperial order to organize a Cabinet, I felt that it was very urgent for the sake of guaranteeing the future progress of the nation to put forth all possible efforts to continue the negotiations with America and bring about a speedy settlement to the China Affair. We have, therefore, exerted ourselves to the utmost in conducting successive conversations with the American Government and have endeavored to bring about a meeting between the President of the United States and myself. The result of these efforts is still pending.

Recently, however, War Minister Tojo has come to believe that there is absolutely no hope of reaching an agreement with America by the time we specified, (namely, the middle or latter part of October), or, in other words, that we should now decide that "there is no reasonable hope to have our demands agreed to" as specified under Section III of the "Plans for the Prosecution of the Imperial Program" which was drawn up at a council in the Imperial Presence on September 6th. He thus concludes that the time has arrived for us to make up our minds to get ready for war against America. However, careful reconsideration of the situation leads me to the conclusion that, given time, the possibility of reaching an agreement with the United States is not hopeless. In particular, I believe that even the most difficult question involved, namely, that of the withdrawal of troops, can be

[17] The *Konoe Memoirs* as reprinted in in U.S. Congress, Joint Committee on the Investigation of the Pearl Harbor Attack, *Hearings* (39 parts, Washington, 1946), part 20, 4025-26.

settled if we are willing to sacrifice our honor to some extent and agree to the formula suggested by America.

To plunge into a great war, the issue of which is most uncertain, at a time when the China Incident is still unsettled would be something which I could not possibly agree to, especially since I have painfully felt my grave responsibility for the present state of affairs ever since the outbreak of the China Incident. It is vitally necessary now, not only to strengthen ourselves for the future but also to set the people's minds at ease, that the Cabinet and the Army and Navy cooperate in the closest possible manner in bringing to a successful conclusion the negotiations with America. Now is the time for us to sacrifice the present for the future and let our people concentrate their entire efforts for the prosperity of the Emperor and the nation.

Thus I have done my utmost in stating my earnest convictions in an endeavor to persuade War Minister Tojo to accept my viewpoint. In response to this, the War Minister insisted that although he greatly appreciated my position and sincerity, it was impossible from the standpoint of preserving military morale for him to agree to the withdrawal of troops; that if we once gave in to America that country would become so arrogant that there would be no end of its depredations; and that even if we should be able to settle the China Affair now, Sino-Japanese relations would again reach a deadlock in a mere two to three years. He pointed out that while there are certain weak points in our position America also has its weak points and that we should therefore grasp the present opportunity and get ready for war at once. I have had four serious conversations with him on this subject but was unable to change his position. It is therefore clear to me that my ideas will not prevail and that I shall be unable to carry out my responsibilities as an advisor to the Throne. I realize that this is entirely due to my insufficiency and I feel very humble as I approach the Throne. It is with trepidation that I present my request, but I humbly and sincerely ask that you relieve me of my present responsibilities.

October 16, 1941   Prince Fumimaro Konoye
                                         Prime Minister

PRINCE KONOE'S MEMORIAL, 1945 [18]

In February, 1945, the Emperor, seriously worried about the way the war was going, held a number of individual conferences with the senior statesmen, that is, the ex-Prime Ministers. When Konoe had his audience with the Emperor, he had made the following frank and somewhat prophetic statement.

Sad though it is, I believe that Japan has already lost the war. Although defeat will be a great stain upon our polity, it need not necessarily occasion undue concern especially since public opinion in America and Britain, on the whole, has not yet gone so far as to demand a fundamental change in our national structure. There are those, of course, who hold extreme views with respect to this question, and it is difficult to predict what changes may take place in public opinion as time passes. From the standpoint of maintaining Japan's imperial system, that which we have most to fear is not defeat itself but, rather, the threat inherent in the possibility that a Communist revolution may accompany defeat. The more I think about it the more I feel that conditions within Japan and those prevailing abroad are rapidly progressing toward such an eventuality.

In the world at large, for instance, there is the prodigious debouchment of the Soviet Union—a development which our people have shallowly tended to underestimate because of the recent dissolution of the Comintern and the earlier adoption by the USSR of a popular

[18] From pp. 47-50, *Japan's Decision to Surrender* (Hoover Library Series Publication No. 24) by Robert J. C. Butow, with the permission of the author and publishers, Stanford University Press. Copyright 1954 by the Board of Trustees of Leland Stanford Junior University. Published under the authority of the Hoover Library on War, Revolution, and Peace.

front, or two-stage-revolution, stratagem. That the Soviet Union has not abandoned her plan to bolshevize the world, however, is manifestly clear from the undisguised mischief-making in which she has recently been engaged in a number of European countries. The fact of the matter is that the Soviet Union has been at pains to establish Soviet regimes in the countries contiguous to her borders and to promote the creation of at least pro-Soviet governments throughout the rest of Europe. In this task, it may be said that she has by and large succeeded.

Although on the surface the Soviet Union stands for the principle of non-intervention in the internal affairs of a state, in actuality she is bent upon the most intensive intervention conceivable in her effort to draw the rest of the world into her orbit. Her goal in the Far East, moreover, is no more nor less than that toward which she is striving in Europe. In Yenan, a Japan Liberation League has been organized around Okano, a Moscow-trained Japanese Communist. This League is collaborating with the Korean Independence Confederation, the Korean Volunteer Army, the Formosan Spearhead Corps, and similar groups in a verbal campaign of propaganda and revolutionary incitement directed at Japan. Such being the case, the danger of Soviet intervention in our own internal affairs in the near future is abundantly great.

The situation within Japan is such that every possible factor favorable to the accomplishment of a Communist revolution is on hand. There is poverty in the life of the people, a rise in the voice of labor, and an expansion of pro-Soviet feeling growing out of an increase in enmity against America and Britain. In addition, there are the actions of the national renovationists—a movement championed by a certain faction within the military, the activities of the so-called "new bureaucrats"—the "fellow-travelers" of this movement, and the secret machinations of the leftists who are pulling the strings from behind.

Of the foregoing factors, that which we have most to fear is the national renovation movement of the militarists. A great number of young military men seem to think that Communism is compatible with Japan's imperial system—a view which, I believe, constitutes the keynote of their renovation argument. I have heard that there are even some members of the imperial family who might lend an ear to their contentions.

Since Japan's professional military men—at least a majority—hail from families below the middle class, their whole environment of life has been such that it is easy for them to fall prey to Communist doctrine. At the same time, however, their military education has thoroughly inculcated them with the spirit of our national polity. The Communist element, therefore, is endeavoring to captivate these militarists with the claim that the national polity and communism can stand side by side.

I believe that it has at length become clear that the Manchurian Incident, the China Incident, and the Greater East Asia War were all perpetrated by the aforementioned national renovation faction of the militarists as part of a purposeful plan. It is a well-known fact that at the time of the trouble in Manchuria the military declared the purpose of the Incident to be internal reform here in Japan. Later on, when the China Incident occurred, one of the central figures of the renovation faction publicly declared, "the longer the Incident lasts, the better, for if a settlement is reached we shall be unable to bring about domestic reform." Although the aim of this national renovation faction within the military may not necessarily be a Communist revolution, I believe that I am not far wrong in saying that the "new bureaucrats" and the sympathizers among the people—who jointly fawn upon these militarists—are consciously harboring the intention of bringing about a Red revolution. It is immaterial whether we call this revolution-minded group right-wing or left-wing, for in reality the right-wingers are nothing more than Communists masquerading in the dress of the national polity-ists. Our ignorant and simple-minded military men are putty in their hands.

What I have said represents the conclusions I have recently reached as a result of having quietly reflected upon the events of the past ten years—years during which I had acquaintances in various quarters: the military, the bureaucracy, the right-wing, and the left-wing. In the light of this conclusion, I now realize that there were a great many things during those years the true meaning of which I have only now come to grasp. Having been honored twice during that period with Your Majesty's command to form a cabinet, I was so eager to do away with friction and conflict within Japan that I acceded to the demands of the national renovationists as much as I could. In my desire to achieve national unity I failed to perceive the real purpose hidden behind the contentions of the extremists. Since there is absolutely no excuse for my lack of foresight, I can only say that I feel gravely responsible for my failure in this respect.

The more critical the war situation becomes, the louder we hear the cry, "One hundred million die together!" Although the so-called right-wingers are the ones who shout the loudest, it is the Communists, in my opinion, who are the instigators of it all, for they hope to achieve their revolutionary aim by taking advantage of the confusion that will arise out of defeat.

While on the one hand there are those who clamor for the utter destruction of America and Britain, an atmosphere seems to be developing, on the other hand, that is favorably disposed toward the Soviet Union. I have been informed that there is even one group of militarists sponsoring a rapprochement with the USSR—a rapprochement at any cost, while others are thinking in terms of an alliance with the Yenan Chinese Communist regime.

Thus, with each passing day the internal and external scene is becoming increasingly favorable to the success of a Communist revolution. If the war situation deteriorates still further, this state of affairs will develop by leaps and bounds.

The question would be different if there were even some slight hope of the fighting taking a turn for the better, but with defeat staring us in the face we shall simply be playing into the hands of the Communists if we elect to continue a war wherein there is no prospect of victory. From the standpoint of preserving the national polity, therefore, I am firmly convinced that we should seek to end the war as speedily as possible.

The greatest obstacle to termination of the conflict is the existence of that group within the military which ever since the Manchurian Incident has driven the country to its present plight. Although the military men have already lost confidence in their ability to prosecute the war to a successful conclusion, they are likely to continue fighting to the very end merely to save face.

Should we endeavor to stop the war abruptly without first rooting out the extremists, I fear that they—supported by sympathizers within both the right- and left-wings—might perpetrate internal disorder thus making it difficult for us to achieve our desired goal. The prerequisite to a termination of the war is therefore the elimination of this extremist element within the military. Once this is done, their followers among the bureaucrats and right- and left-wing segments of the people will also fade away, for the latter have not as yet attained an independent influence of their own but have merely tried to achieve their aims by marching behind the militarists and using the latter to their advantage. Thus, if the tree is struck at the roots, its leaves and branches will wither and die of their own accord.

This may be slightly wishful thinking, but, if the extremist group is purged, is it not possible that the character of the army will so change that the atmosphere in America, Britain, and Chungking may improve somewhat? The Allied war aim is the overthrow of Japan's military clique, but if the character and policy of our military undergo a fundamental change the Allies may be moved to give careful consideration to the question of continuing the war.

At any rate, the reconstruction of the military through the elimination of the extremists is the prerequisite to saving Japan from a Communist revolution. I must therefore urge Your Majesty to make a bold decision toward that end.

THE 1947 CONSTITUTION[19]

It will be noted that the 1947 Constitution is almost twice as long as the Meiji Constitution. This reflects the desire of the framers to be as explicit as possible and leave nothing to chance. Following is the complete text.

We, the Japanese people, acting through our duly elected representatives in the National Diet, determined that we shall secure for ourselves and our posterity the fruits of peaceful cooperation with all nations and the blessings of liberty throughout this land, and resolved that never again shall we be visited with the horrors of war through the action of government, do proclaim that sovereign power resides with the people and do firmly establish this Constitution. Government is a sacred trust of the people, the authority for which is derived from the people, the powers of which are exercised by the representatives of the people, and the benefits of which are enjoyed by the people. This is a universal principle of mankind upon which this Constitution is founded. We reject and revoke all constitutions, laws, ordinances, and rescripts in conflict herewith.

We, the Japanese people, desire peace for all time and are deeply conscious of the high ideals controlling human relationship, and we have determined to preserve our security and existence, trusting in the justice and faith of the peace-loving peoples of the world. We desire to occupy an honored place in an international society striving for the preservation of peace, and the banishment of tyranny and slavery, oppression and intolerance for all time from the earth. We recognize that all peoples of the world have the right to live in peace, free from fear and want.

[19] Department of State Publication 2836, Far Eastern Series 22 (Washington, 1947).

We believe that no nation is responsible to itself alone, but that laws of political morality are universal; and that obedience to such laws is incumbent upon all nations who would sustain their own sovereignty and justify their sovereign relationship with other nations.

We, the Japanese people, pledge our national honor to accomplish these high ideals and purposes with all our resources.

Chapter 1. The Emperor

ARTICLE 1. The Emperor shall be the symbol of the State and of the unity of the people, deriving his position from the will of the people with whom resides sovereign power.

ARTICLE 2. The Imperial Throne shall be dynastic and succeeded to in accordance with the Imperial House Law passed by the Diet.

ARTICLE 3. The advice and approval of the Cabinet shall be required for all acts of the Emperor in matters of state, and the Cabinet shall be responsible therefor.

ARTICLE 4. The Emperor shall perform only such acts in matters of state as are provided for in this Constitution and he shall not have powers related to government.

The Emperor may delegate the performance of his acts in matters of state as may be provided by law.

ARTICLE 5. When, in accordance with the Imperial House Law, a Regency is established, the Regent shall perform his acts in matters of state in the Emperor's name. In this case, paragraph one of the preceding article will be applicable.

ARTICLE 6.   The Emperor shall appoint the Prime Minister as designated by the Diet.

The Emperor shall appoint the Chief Judge of the Supreme Court as designated by the Cabinet.

ARTICLE 7. The Emperor, with the advice and approval of the Cabinet, shall perform the following acts in matters of state on behalf of the people:

Promulgation of amendments of the constitution, laws, cabinet orders and treaties.

Convocation of the Diet.

Dissolution of the House of Representatives.

Proclamation of general election of members of the Diet.

Attestation of the appointment and dismissal of Ministers of State and other officials as provided for by law, and of full powers and credentials of Ambassadors and Ministers.

Attestation of general and special amnesty, commutation of punishment, reprieve, and restoration of rights.

Awarding of honors.

Attestation of instruments of ratification and other diplomatic documents as provided for by law.

Receiving foreign ambassadors and ministers.

Performance of ceremonial functions.

ARTICLE 8. No property can be given to, or received by, the Imperial House, nor can an gifts be made therefrom, without the authorization of the Diet.

Chapter II. Renunciation of War

ARTICLE 9. Aspiring sincerely to an international peace based on justice and order, the Japanese people forever renounce war as a sovereign right of the nation and the threat or use of force as means of settling international disputes.

In order to accomplish the aim of the preceding paragraph, land, sea, and air forces, as well as other war potential, will never be maintained. The right of belligerency of the state will not be recognized.

Chapter III. Rights and Duties of the People

ARTICLE 10. The conditions necessary for being a Japanese national shall be determined by law.

ARTICLE 11. The people shall not be prevented from enjoying any of the fundamental human rights. These fundamental human rights guaranteed to the people by this Constitution shall be conferred upon the people of this and future generations as eternal and inviolate rights.

ARTICLE 12. The freedoms and rights guaranteed to the people by this Constitution shall be maintained by the constant endeavor of the people, who shall refrain from any abuse of these freedoms and rights and shall always be responsible for utilizing them for the public welfare.

ARTICLE 13. All of the people shall be respected as individuals. Their right to life, liberty, and the pursuit of happiness shall, to the extent that it does not interfere with the public welfare, be the supreme consideration in legislation and in other governmental affairs.

ARTICLE 14. All of the people are equal under the law and there shall be no discrimination in political, economic or social relations because of race, creed, sex, social status or family origin.

Peers and peerage shall not be recognized.

No privilege shall accompany any award of honor, decoration or any distinction, nor shall any such award be valid beyond the lifetime of the individual who now holds or hereafter may receive it.

ARTICLE 15. The people have the inalienable right to choose their public officials and to dismiss them.

All public officials are servants of the whole community and not of any group thereof.

Universal adult suffrage is guaranteed with regard to the election of public officials.

In all elections, secrecy of the ballot shall not be violated. A voter shall not be answerable, publicly or privately, for the choice he has made.

ARTICLE 16. Every person shall have the right of peaceful petition for the redress of damage, for the removal of public officials, for the enactment, repeal or amendment of laws, ordinances or regulations and for other matters; nor shall any person be in any way discriminated against for sponsoring such a petition.

ARTICLE 17. Every person may sue for redress as provided by law from the State or a public entity, in case he has suffered damage through illegal act of any public official.

ARTICLE 18. No person shall be held in bondage of any kind. Involuntary servitude, except as punishment for crime, is prohibited.

ARTICLE 19. Freedom of thought and conscience shall not be violated.

ARTICLE 20. Freedom of religion is guaranteed to all.

No religious organization shall receive any privileges from the State, nor exercise any political authority.

No person shall be compelled to take part in any religious act, celebration, rite or practice.

The State and its organs shall refrain from religious education or any other religious activity.

ARTICLE 21. Freedom of assembly and association as well as speech, press and all other forms of expression are guaranteed.

No censorship shall be maintained, nor shall the secrecy of any means of communication be violated.

ARTICLE 22. Every person shall have freedom to choose and change his residence and to choose his occupation to the extent that it does not interfere with the public welfare.

Freedom of all persons to move to a foreign country and to divest themselves of their nationality shall be inviolate.

ARTICLE 23. Academic freedom is guaranteed.

ARTICLE 24. Marriage shall be based only on the mutual consent of both sexes and it shall be maintained through mutual cooperation with the equal rights of husband and wife as a basis.

With regard to choice of spouse, property rights, inheritance, choice of domicile, divorce and other matters pertaining to marriage and the family, laws shall be enacted from the standpoint of individual dignity and the essential equality of the sexes.

ARTICLE 25. All people shall have the right to maintain the minimum standards of wholesome and cultured living.

In all spheres of life, the State shall use its endeavors for the promotion and extension of social welfare and security, and of public health.

ARTICLE 26. All people shall have the right to receive an equal education correspondent to their ability, as provided by law.

All people shall be obligated to have all boys and girls under their protection receive ordinary education as provided for by law. Such compulsory education shall be free.

ARTICLE 27. All people shall have the right and the obligation to work.

Standards for wages, hours, rest and other working conditions shall be fixed by law.

Children shall not be exploited.

ARTICLE 28. The right of workers to organize and to bargain and act collectively is guaranteed.

ARTICLE 29. The right to own or to hold property is inviolable.

Property rights shall be defined by law, in conformity with the public welfare.

Private property may be taken for public use upon just compensation therefor.

ARTICLE 30. The people shall be liable to taxation as provided by law.

ARTICLE 31. No person shall be deprived of life or liberty, nor shall any other criminal penalty be imposed, except according to procedure established by law.

ARTICLE 32. No person shall be denied the right of access to the courts.

ARTICLE 33. No person shall be apprehended except upon warrant issued by competent judicial officer which specifies the offense with which the person is charged, unless he is apprehended, the offense being committed.

ARTICLE 34. No person shall be arrested or detained without being at once informed of the charges against him or without the immediate privilege of counsel; nor shall he be detained without adequate cause; and upon demand of any person such cause must be immediately shown in open court in his presence and the presence of his counsel.

ARTICLE 35. The right of all persons to be secure in their homes, papers and effects against entries, searches and seizures shall not be impaired except upon warrant issued for adequate cause and particularly describing the place to be searched and things to be seized, or except as provided by ARTICLE 33.

Each search or seizure shall be made upon separate warrant issued by a competent judicial officer.

ARTICLE 36. The infliction of torture by any public officer and cruel punishments are absolutely forbidden.

ARTICLE 37. In all criminal cases the accused shall

enjoy the right to a speedy and public trial by an impartial tribunal.

He shall be permitted full opportunity to examine all witnesses, and he shall have the right of compulsory process for obtaining witnesses on his behalf at public expense.

At all times the accused shall have the assistance of competent counsel who shall, if the accused is unable to secure the same by his own efforts, be assigned to his use by the State.

ARTICLE 38. No person shall be compelled to testify against himself.

Confession made under compulsion, torture or threat, or after prolonged arrest or detention shall not be admitted in evidence.

No person shall be convicted or punished in cases where the only proof against him is his own confession.

ARTICLE 39. No person shall be held criminally liable for an act which was lawful at the time it was committed, or of which he has been acquitted, nor shall he be placed in double jeopardy.

ARTICLE 40. Any person, in case he is acquitted after he has been arrested or detained, may sue the State for redress as provided by law.

Chapter IV. The Diet

ARTICLE 41. The Diet shall be the highest organ of state power, and shall be the sole law-making organ of the State.

ARTICLE 42. The Diet shall consist of two Houses, namely the House of Representatives and the House of Councillors.

ARTICLE 43. Both Houses shall consist of elected members, representative of all the people.

The number of the members of each House shall be fixed by law.

ARTICLE 44. The qualifications of members of both Houses and their electors shall be fixed by law. However, there shall be no discrimination because of race, creed, sex, social status, family origin, education, property or income.

ARTICLE 45. The term of office of members of the

House of Representatives shall be four years. However, the term shall be terminated before the full term is up in case the House of Representatives is dissolved.

ARTICLE 46. The term of office of members of the House of Councillors shall be six years, and election for half the members shall take place every three years.

ARTICLE 47. Electoral districts, method of voting and other matters pertaining to the method of election of members of both Houses shall be fixed by law.

ARTICLE 48. No person shall be permitted to be a member of both Houses simultaneously.

ARTICLE 49. Members of both Houses shall receive appropriate annual payment from the national treasury in accordance with law.

ARTICLE 50. Except in cases provided by law, members of both Houses shall be exempt from apprehension while the Diet is in session, and any members apprehended before the opening of the session shall be freed during the term of the session upon demand of the House.

ARTICLE 51. Members of both Houses shall not be held liable outside the House for speeches, debates or votes cast inside the House.

ARTICLE 52. An ordinary session of the Diet shall be convoked once per year.

ARTICLE 53. The Cabinet may determine to convoke extraordinary sessions of the Diet. When a quarter or more of the total members of either House makes the demand, the Cabinet must determine on such convocation.

ARTICLE 54. When the House of Representatives is dissolved, there must be a general election of members of the House of Representatives within forty (40) days from the date of dissolution, and the Diet must be convoked within thirty (30) days from the date of the election.

When the House of Representatives is dissolved, the House of Councillors is closed at the same time. However, the Cabinet may in time of national emergency convoke the House of Councillors in emergency session.

Measures taken at such session as mentioned in the proviso of the preceding paragraph shall be provisional and shall become null and void unless agreed to by the House of Representatives within a period of ten (10) days after the opening of the next session of the Diet.

ARTICLE 55. Each House shall judge disputes related to qualifications of its members. However, in order to deny a seat to any member, it is necessary to pass a resolution by a majority of two-thirds or more of the members present.

ARTICLE 56. Business cannot be transacted in either House unless one-third or more of total membership is present.

All matters shall be decided, in each House, by a majority of those present, except as elsewhere provided in the Constitution, and in case of a tie, the presiding officer shall decide the issue.

ARTICLE 57. Deliberation in each House shall be public. However, a secret meeting may be held where a majority of two-thirds or more of those members present passes a resolution therefor.

Each House shall keep a record of proceedings. This record shall be published and given general circulation, excepting such parts of proceedings of secret session as may be deemed to require secrecy.

Upon demand of one-fifth or more of the members present, votes of the members on any matter shall be recorded in the minutes.

ARTICLE 58. Each House shall select its own president and other officials.

Each House shall establish its rules pertaining to meetings, proceedings and internal discipline, and may punish members for disorderly conduct. However, in order to expel a member, a majority of two-thirds or more of those members present must pass a resolution thereon.

ARTICLE 59. A bill becomes a law on passage by both Houses, except as otherwise provided by the Constitution.

A bill which is passed by the House of Representatives, and upon which the House of Councillors makes a decision different from that of the House of Representatives, becomes a law when passed a second time by the House of Representatives by a majority of two-thirds or more of the members present.

The provision of the preceding paragraph does not preclude the House of Representatives from calling for the meeting of a joint committee of both Houses, provided for by law.

Failure by the House of Councillors to take final action within sixty (60) days after receipt of a bill passed by the House of Representatives, time in recess excepted, may be determined by the House of Representatives to constitute a rejection of the said bill by the House of Councillors.

ARTICLE 60. The budget must first be submitted to the House of Representatives.

Upon consideration of the budget, when the House of Councillors makes a decision different from that of the House of Representatives, and when no agreement can be reached even through a joint committee of both Houses, provided for by law, or in the case of failure by the House of Councillors to take final action within thirty (30) days, the period of recess excluded, after the receipt of the budget passed by the House of Representatives, the decision of the House of Representatives shall be the decision of the Diet.

ARTICLE 61. The second paragraph of the preceding article applies also to the Diet approval required for the conclusion of treaties.

ARTICLE 62. Each House may conduct investigations in relation to government, and may demand the presence and testimony of witnesses, and the production of records.

ARTICLE 63. The Prime Minister and other Ministers of State may, at any time, appear in either House for the purpose of speaking on bills, regardless of whether they are members of the House or not. They must appear when their presence is required in order to give answers or explanations.

ARTICLE 64. The Diet shall set up an impeachment court from among the members of both Houses for the purpose of trying those judges against whom removal proceedings have been instituted.

Matters relating to impeachment shall be provided by law.

Chapter V. The Cabinet

ARTICLE 65. Executive power shall be vested in the Cabinet.

ARTICLE 66. The Cabinet shall consist of the Prime Minister, who shall be its head, and other Ministers of State, as provided for by law.

The Prime Minister and other Ministers of State must be civilians.

The Cabinet, in the exercise of executive power, shall be collectively responsible to the Diet.

ARTICLE 67. The Prime Minister shall be designated from among the members of the Diet by a resolution of the Diet. This designation shall precede all other business.

If the House of Representatives and the House of Councillors disagree and if no agreement can be reached even through a joint committee of both Houses, provided for by law, or the House of Councillors fails to make designation within ten (10) days, exclusive of the period of recess, after the House of Representatives has made designation, the decision of the House of Representatives shall be the decision of the Diet.

ARTICLE 68. The Prime Minister shall appoint the Ministers of State. However, a majority of their number must be chosen from among the members of the Diet.

The Prime Minister may remove the Ministers of State as he chooses.

ARTICLE 69. If the House of Representatives passes a non-confidence resolution, or rejects a confidence resolution, the Cabinet shall resign en masse, unless the House of Representatives is dissolved within ten (10) days.

ARTICLE 70. When there is a vacancy in the post of Prime Minister, or upon the first convocation of the Diet after a general election of members of the House of Representatives, the Cabinet shall resign en masse.

ARTICLE 71. In the cases mentioned in the two preceding articles, the Cabinet shall continue its functions until the time when a new Prime Minister is appointed.

ARTICLE 72. The Prime Minister, representing the Cabinet, submits bills, reports on general national affairs and foreign relations to the Diet and exercises control and supervision over various administrative branches.

ARTICLE 73. The Cabinet, in addition to other general administrative functions, shall perform the following functions:

Administer the law faithfully; conduct affairs of state. Manage foreign affairs.

Conclude treaties. However, it shall obtain prior or, depending on circumstances, subsequent approval of the Diet.

Administer the civil service, in accordance with standards established by law.

Prepare the budget, and present it to the Diet.

Enact cabinet orders in order to execute the provisions of this Constitution and of the law. However, it cannot include penal provisions in such cabinet orders unless authorized by such law.

Decide on general amnesty, special amnesty, commutation of punishment, reprieve, and restoration of rights.

ARTICLE. 74. All laws and cabinet orders shall be signed by the competent Minister of State and countersigned by the Prime Minister.

ARTICLE 75. The Ministers of State, during their tenure of office, shall not be subject to legal action without the consent of the Prime Minister. However, the right to take that action is not impaired hereby.

Chapter VI. Judiciary

ARTICLE 76. The whole judicial power is vested in a Supreme Court and in such inferior courts as are established by law.

No extraordinary tribunal shall be established, nor shall any organ or agency of the Executive be given final judicial power.

All judges shall be independent in the exercise of their conscience and shall be bound only by this Constitution and the laws.

ARTICLE 77. The Supreme Court is vested with the rule-making power under which it determines the rules of procedure and of practice, and of matters relating to attorneys, the internal discipline of the courts and the administration of judicial affairs.

Public procurators shall be subject to the rule-making power of the Supreme Court.

The Supreme Court may delegate the power to make rules for inferior courts to such courts.

ARTICLE 78. Judges shall not be removed except by public impeachment unless judicially declared mentally or physically incompetent to perform official duties. No disciplinary action against judges shall be administered by any executive organ or agency.

ARTICLE 79. The Supreme Court shall consist of a Chief Judge and such number of judges as may be determined by law; all such judges excepting the Chief Judge shall be appointed by the Cabinet.

The appointment of the judges of the Supreme Court shall be reviewed by the people at the first general election of members of the House of Representatives following their appointment, and shall be reviewed again at the first general election of members of the House of Representatives after a lapse of ten (10) years, and in the same manner thereafter.

In cases mentioned in the foregoing paragraph, when the majority of the voters favors the dismissal of a judge, he shall be dismissed.

Matters pertaining to review shall be prescribed by law.

The judges of the Supreme Court shall be retired upon the attainment of the age as fixed by law.

All such judges shall receive, at regular stated intervals, adequate compensation which shall not be decreased during their terms of office.

ARTICLE 80. The judges of the inferior courts shall be appointed by the Cabinet from a list of persons nominated by the Supreme Court. All such judges shall hold office for a term of ten (10) years with privilege of reappointment, provided that they shall be retired upon the attainment of the age as fixed by law.

The judges of the inferior courts shall receive, at regular stated intervals, adequate compensation which shall not be decreased during their terms of office.

ARTICLE 81. The Supreme Court is the court of last

resort with power to determine the constitutionality of any law, order, regulation or official act.

ARTICLE 82. Trials shall be conducted and judgment declared publicly.

Where a court unanimously determines publicity to be dangerous to public order or morals, a trial may be conducted privately, but trials of political offenses, offenses involving the press or cases wherein the rights of people as guaranteed in Chapter III of this Constitution are in question shall always be conducted publicly.

Chapter VII. Finance

ARTICLE 83. The power to administer national finances shall be exercised as the Diet shall determine.

ARTICLE 84. No new taxes shall be imposed or existing ones modified except by law or under such conditions as law may prescribe.

ARTICLE 85. No money shall be expended, nor shall the State obligate itself, except as authorized by the Diet.

ARTICLE 86. The Cabinet shall prepare and submit to the Diet for its consideration and decision a budget for each fiscal year.

ARTICLE 87. In order to provide for unforeseen deficiencies in the budget, a reserve fund may be authorized by the Diet to be expended upon the responsibility of the Cabinet.

The Cabinet must get subsequent approval of the Diet for all payments from the reserve fund.

ARTICLE 88. All property of the Imperial Household shall belong to the State. All expenses of the Imperial Household shall be appropriated by the Diet in the budget.

ARTICLE 89. No public money or other property shall be expended or appropriated for the use, benefit or maintenance of any religious institution or association, or for any charitable, educational or benevolent enterprises not under the control of public authority.

ARTICLE 90. Final accounts of the expenditures and revenues of the State shall be audited annually by a Board of Audit and submitted by the Cabinet to the Diet, together with the statement of audit, during the fiscal year immediately following the period covered.

The organization and competency of the Board of Audit shall be determined by law.

ARTICLE 91. At regular intervals and at least annually the Cabinet shall report to the Diet and the people on the state of national finances.

Chapter VIII. Local Self-Government

ARTICLE 92. Regulations concerning organization and operations of local public entities shall be fixed by law in accordance with the principle of local autonomy.

ARTICLE 93. The local public entities shall establish assemblies as their deliberate organs, in accordance with law.

The chief executive officers of all local public entities, the members of their assemblies, and such other local officials as may be determined by law shall be elected by direct popular vote within their several communities.

ARTICLE 94. Local public entities shall have the right to manage their property, affairs and administration and to enact their own regulations within law.

ARTICLE 95. A special law, applicable only to one local public entity, cannot be enacted by the Diet without the consent of the majority of the voters of the local public entity concerned, obtained in accordance with law.

Chapter IX. Amendments

ARTICLE 96. Amendments to this Constitution shall be initiated by the Diet, through a concurring vote of two-thirds or more of all the members of each House and shall thereupon be submitted to the people for ratification, which shall require the affirmative vote of a majority of all votes cast thereon, at a special referedum or at such election as the Diet shall specify.

Amendments when so ratified shall immediately be promulgated by the Emperor in the name of the people, as an integral part of this Constitution.

Chapter X. Supreme Law

ARTICLE 97. The fundamental human rights by this Constitution guaranteed to the people of Japan are fruits of the age-old struggle of man to be free; they have survived the many exacting tests for durability and are conferred upon this and future generations in trust, to be held for all time inviolate.

ARTICLE 98. This Constitution shall be the supreme law of the nation and no law, ordinance, imperial rescript or other act of government, or part thereof, contrary to the provisions hereof, shall have legal force or validity.

The treaties concluded by Japan and established laws of nations shall be faithfully observed.

ARTICLE 99. The Emperor or the Regent as well as Ministers of State, members of the Diet, judges, and all other public officials have the obligation to respect and uphold this Constitution.

Chapter XI. Supplementary Provisions

ARTICLE 100. This Constitution shall be enforced as from the day when the period of six months will have elapsed counting from the day of its promulgation.

The enactment of laws necessary for the enforcement of this Constitution, the election of members of the House of Councillors and the procedure for the convocation of the Diet and other preparatory procedures necessary for the enforcement of this Constitution may be executed before the day prescribed in the preceding paragraph.

ARTICLE 101. If the House of Councillors is not constituted before the effective date of this Constitution, the House of Representatives shall function as the Diet until such time as the House of Councillors shall be constituted.

ARTICLE 102. The term of office for half the members of the House of Councillors serving in the first term under this Constitution shall be three years. Members falling under this category shall be determined in accordance with law.

ARTICLE 103. The Ministers of State, members of the House of Representatives and judges in office on the effective date of this Constitution, and all other public officials who occupy positions corresponding to such positions as are recognized by this Constitution shall not forfeit their positions automatically on account of the enforcement of this Constitution unless otherwise specified by law. When, however, successors are elected or appointed under the provisions of this Constitution, they shall forfeit their positions as a matter of course.

TREATY OF PEACE, 1951 [20]

As early as March 17, 1947, General Douglas Mac-Arthur expressed his belief that Japan was ready for a peace treaty. Later that same year the United States Government attempted to arrange a preliminary conference, but the U.S.S.R. and China objected to the procedures which were to be used. As a result the project was dropped. A peace treaty only became possible when the United States decided to avoid the conference method and use traditional diplomatic processes.

Treaty of Peace Between the Allied Powers and Japan

Whereas the Allied Powers and Japan are resolved that henceforth their relations shall be those of nations which, as sovereign equals, cooperate in friendly association to promote to their common welfare and to maintain international peace and security, and are therefore desirous of concluding a Treaty of Peace which will settle questions still outstanding as a result of the existence of a state of war between them;

Whereas Japan for its part declares its intention to apply for membership in the United Nations and in all circumstances to conform to the principles of the Charter of the United Nations; to strive to realize the objectives of the Universal Declaration of Human Rights; to seek to create within Japan conditions of stability and well-being as defined in Articles 55 and 56 of the Charter of the United Nations and already initiated by post-surrender Japanese legislation; and in public and private trade and commerce to conform to internationally accepted fair practices;

[20] Department of State Publication 4613, Treaties and Other International Acts Series 2490 (Washington, 1952), pp. 5-25.

Whereas the Allied Powers welcome the intentions of Japan set out in the foregoing paragraph;

The Allied Powers and Japan have therefore determined to conclude the present Treaty of Peace, and have accordingly appointed the undersigned Plenipotentiaries, who, after presentation of their full powers, found in good and due form, have agreed on the following provisions:

Chapter I. Peace

ARTICLE 1. (a) The state of war between Japan and each of the Allied Powers is terminated as from the date on which the present Treaty comes into force between Japan and the Allied Power concerned as provided for in Article 23.

(b) The Allied Powers recognize the full sovereignty of the Japanese people over Japan and its territorial waters.

Chapter II. Territory

ARTICLE 2. (a) Japan, recognizing the independence of Korea, renounces all right, title and claim to Korea, including the islands of Quelpart, Port Hamilton and Dagelet.

(b) Japan renounces all right, title and claim to Formosa and the Pescadores.

(c) Japan renounces all right, title and claim to the Kurile Islands, and to that portion of Sakhalin and the islands adjacent to it over which Japan acquired sovereignty as a consequence of the Treaty of Portsmouth of September 5, 1905.

(d) Japan renounces all right, title and claim in connection with the League of Nations Mandate System, and accepts the action of the United Nations Security Council of April 2, 1947, extending the trusteeship system to the Pacific Islands formerly under mandate to Japan.

(e) Japan renounces all claim to any right or title to or interest in connection with any part of the Antarctic area, whether deriving from the activities of Japanese nationals or otherwise.

(f) Japan renounces all right, title and claim to the Spratly Islands and to the Paracel Islands.

ARTICLE 3. Japan will concur in any proposal of the United States to the United Nations to place under its trusteeship system, with the United States as the sole administering authority, Nansei Shoto south of 29° north latitude (including the Ryukyu Islands and the Daito Islands), Nanpo Shoto south of Sofu Gan (including the Bonin Islands, Rosario Island and the Volcano Islands) and Parece Vela and Marcus Island. Pending the making of such a proposal and affirmative action thereon, the United States will have the right to exercise all and any powers of administration, legislation and jurisdiction over the territory and inhabitants of these islands, including their territoral waters. . . .

(*Article 4 deals with dispositions of property.*)

Chapter III. Security

ARTICLE 5. (a) Japan accepts the obligations set forth in ARTICLE 2 of the Charter of the United Nations, and in particular the obligations

(i) to settle its international disputes by peaceful means in such a manner that international peace and security, and justice, are not endangered;

(ii) to refrain in its international relations from the threat or use of force against the territorial integrity or political independence of any State or in any other manner inconsistent with the Purposes of the United Nations;

(iii) to give the United Nations every assistance in any action it takes in accordance with the Charter and to refrain from giving assistance to any State against which the United Nations may take preventive or enforcement action.

(b) The Allied Powers confirm that they will be guided by the principles of ARTICLE 2 of the Charter of the United Nations in their relations with Japan.

(c) The Allied Powers for their part recognize that Japan as a sovereign nation possesses the inherent right of individual or collective self-defense referred to in Article 51 of the Charter of the United Nations and that Japan may voluntarily enter into collective security arrangements.

ARTICLE 6. (a) All occupation forces of the Allied Powers shall be withdrawn from Japan as soon as possible after the coming into force of the present Treaty, and in any case not later than 90 days thereafter. Nothing in this provision shall, however, prevent the stationing or retention of foreign armed forces in Japanese territory under or in consequence of any bilateral or multilateral agreements which have been or may be made between one or more of the Allied Powers, on the one hand, and Japan on the other.

(b) The provisions of ARTICLE 9 of the Potsdam Proclamation of July 26, 1945, dealing with the return of Japanese military forces to their homes, to the extent not already completed, will be carried out.

(c) All Japanese property for which compensation has not already been paid, which was supplied for the use of the occupation forces and which remains in the possession of those forces at the time of the coming into force of the present Treaty, shall be returned to the Japanese Government within the same 90 days unless other arrangements are made by mutual agreement.

Chapter IV. Political and Economic Clauses

ARTICLE 7. (a) Each of the Allied Powers, within one year after the present Treaty has come into force between it and Japan, will notify Japan which of its prewar bilateral treaties or conventions with Japan it wishes to continue in force or revive, and any treaties or conventions so notified shall continue in force or be revived subject only to such amendments as may be necessary to ensure conformity with the present Treaty. The treaties and conventions so notified shall be considered as having been continued in force or revived three months after the date of notification and shall be registered with the Secretariat of the United Nations. All such treaties and conventions as to which Japan is not so notified shall be regarded as abrogated.

(b) Any notification made under paragraph (a) of this Article may except from the operation or revival of a treaty or convention any territory for the international relations of which the notifying Power is responsible, until three months after the date on which notice is given to Japan that such exception shall cease to apply.

ARTICLE 8. (a) Japan will recognize the full force of all treaties now or hereafter concluded by the Allied Powers for terminating the state of war initiated on September 1, 1939, as well as any other arrangements by the Allied Powers for or in connection with the restoration of peace. Japan also accepts the arrangements made for terminating the former League of Nations and Permanent Court of International Justice.

(b) Japan renounces all such rights and interests as it may derive from being a signatory power of the Conventions of St. Germain-en-Laye of September 10, 1919, and the Straits Agreement of Montreux of July 20, 1936 and from Article 16 of the Treaty of Peace with Turkey signed at Lausanne on July 24, 1923.

(c) Japan renounces all rights, title and interests acquired under, and is discharged from all obligations resulting from the Agreement between Germany and the Creditor Powers of January 20, 1930, and its Annexes, including the Trust Agreement, dated May 17, 1930; the Convention of January 20, 1930, respecting the Bank for International Settlements; and the Statutes of the Bank for International Settlements. Japan will notify to the Ministry of Foreign Affairs in Paris within six months of the first coming into force of the present Treaty its renunciation of the rights, title and interests referred to in this paragraph.

ARTICLE 9. Japan will enter promptly into negotiations with the Allied Powers so desiring for the conclusion of bilateral and multilateral agreements providing for the regulation or limitation of fishing and the conservation and development of fisheries on the high sea.

ARTICLE 10. Japan renounces all special rights and interests in China, including all benefits and privileges resulting from the provisions of the final Protocol signed at Peking on September 7, 1901, and all annexes, notes and documents supplementary thereto, and agrees to the abrogation in respect to Japan of the said protocol, annexes, notes and documents.

ARTICLE 11. Japan accepts the judgments of the International Military Tribunal for the Far East and of other Allied War Crimes Courts both within and outside Japan, and will carry out the sentences imposed thereby upon Japanese nationals imprisoned in Japan. The power to grant clemency, to reduce sentences and to parole with respect to such prisoners may not be exercised except on the decision of the Government or Governments which imposed the sentence in each instance, and on the recommendation of Japan. In the case of persons sentenced by the International Military Tribunal for the Far East, such power may not be exercised except on the decision of a majority of the Governments represented on the Tribunal, and on the recommendation of Japan.

ARTICLE 12. (a) Japan declares its readiness promptly to enter into negotiations for the conclusion with each of the Allied Powers of treaties or agreements to place their trading, maritime and other commercial relations on a stable and friendly basis.

(b) Pending the conclusion of the relevant treaty or agreement, Japan will, during a period of four years from the first coming into force of the present Treaty

(1) Accord to each of the Allied Powers, its nationals, products and vessels

   (i) most-favored-nation treatment with respect to customs duties, charges, restrictions and other regulations on or in connection with the importation and exportation of goods;

  (ii) national treatment with respect to shipping, navigation and imported goods, and with respect to natural and juridical persons and their interests—such treatment to include all matters pertaining to the levying and collection of taxes, access to the courts, the making and performance of contracts, rights to property (tangible and intangible), participation in juridical entities constituted under Japanese law, and generally the conduct of all kinds of business and professional activities;

(2) ensure that external purchase and sales of Japanese state trading enterprises shall be based solely on commercial considerations.

(c) In respect to any matter, however, Japan shall be obliged to accord to an Allied Power national treatment, or most-favored-nation treatment, only to the extent that the Allied Power concerned accords Japan national treatment or most-favored-nation treatment, as the case may be, in respect of the same matter. The reciprocity envisaged in the foregoing sentence shall be determined, in the case of products, vessels and juridical entities of, and persons domiciled in, any non-metropolitan territory of an Allied Power, and in the case of juridical entities of, and persons domiciled in, any state or province of an Allied Power having a federal government, by reference to the treatment accorded to Japan in such territory, state or province.

(d) In the application of this Article, a discriminatory measure shall not be considered to derogate from the grant of national or most-favored-nation treatment, as the case may be, if such measure is based on an exception customarily provided for in the commercial treaties of the party applying it, or on the need to safeguard that party's external financial position or balance of payments (except in respect to shipping and navigation), or on the need to maintain its essential security interests, and provided such measure is proportionate to the circumstances and not applied in an arbitrary or unreasonable manner.

(e) Japan's obligations under this Article shall not be affected by the exercise of any Allied rights under Article 14 of the present Treaty; nor shall the provisions of this Article be understood as limiting the undertakings assumed by Japan by virtue of Article 15 of the Treaty.

ARTICLE 13. (a) Japan will enter into negotiations with any of the Allied Powers, promptly upon the request of such Power or Powers, for the conclusion of bilateral or multilateral agreements relating to international civil air transport.

(b) Pending the conclusion of such agreement or agreements, Japan will, during a period of four years from the first coming into force of the present Treaty, extend to such Power treatment not less favorable with respect to air-traffic rights and privileges than those exercised by any such Powers at the date of such coming into force, and will accord complete equality of opportunity in respect to the operation and development of air services.

(c) Pending its becoming a party to the Convention on International Civil Aviation in accordance with Article 93 thereof, Japan will give effect to the provisions of that Convention applicable to the international navigation of aircraft, and will give effect to the standards, practices and procedures adopted as annexes to the Convention in accordance with the terms of the Convention. . . .

(*Articles 14-21 deal with claims and property.*)

Chapter VI. Settlement of Disputes

ARTICLE 22. If in the opinion of any Party to the present Treaty there has arisen a dispute concerning the interpretation or execution of the Treaty, which is not settled by reference to a special claims tribunal or by other agreed means, the dispute shall, at the request of any party thereto, be referred for decision to the International Court of Justice. Japan and those Allied Powers which are not already parties to the Statute of the International Court of Justice will deposit with the Registrar of the Court, at the time of their respective ratifications of the present Treaty, and in conformity with the resolution of the United Nations Security Council, dated October 15, 1946, a general declaration accepting the jurisdiction, without special agreement, of the Court generally in respect to all disputes of the character referred to in this Article.

Chapter VII. Final Clauses

ARTICLE 23. (a) The present Treaty shall be ratified by the States which sign it, including Japan, and will come into force for all the States which have then ratified it, when instruments of ratification have been deposited by Japan and by a majority, including the United States of America as the principal occupying Power, of the following States, namely Australia, Canada, Ceylon, France, Indonesia, the Kingdom of the Netherlands, New Zealand, Pakistan, the Republic of the Philippines, the United Kingdom of Great Britain and Northern Ireland,

and the United States of America. The present Treaty shall come into force for each State which subsequently ratifies it, on the date of the deposit of its instrument of ratification.

(b) If the Treaty has not come into force within nine months after the date of the deposit of Japan's ratification, any State which has ratified it may bring the Treaty into force between itself and Japan by a notification to that effect given to the Governments of Japan and the United States of America not later than three years after the date of deposit of Japan's ratification.

ARTICLE 24. All instruments of ratification shall be deposited with the Government of the United States of America which will notify all the signatory States of each such deposit, of the date of the coming into force of the Treaty under paragraph (a) of ARTICLE 23, and of any notifications made under paragraph (b) of ARTICLE 23.

ARTICLE 25. For purposes of the present Treaty the Allied Powers shall be the States at war with Japan, or any State which previously formed a part of the territory of a State named in ARTICLE 23, provided that in each case the State concerned has signed and ratified the Treaty. Subject to the provisions of ARTICLE 21, the present Treaty shall not confer any rights, titles or benefits on any State which is not an Allied Power as herein defined; nor shall any right, title or interest of Japan be deemed to be diminished or prejudiced by any provision of the Treaty in favor of a State which is not an Allied Power as so defined.

ARTICLE 26. Japan will be prepared to conclude with any State which signed or adhered to the United Nations Declaration of January 1, 1942, and which is at war with Japan, or with any State which previously formed a part of the territory of a State named in ARTICLE 23, which is not a signatory of the present Treaty, a bilateral Treaty of Peace on the same or substantially the same terms as are provided for in the present Treaty, but this obligation on the part of Japan will expire three years after the first coming into force of the present Treaty. Should Japan make a peace settlement or war claims settlement with any State granting that State greater advantages than those provided by the present Treaty, those same advantages shall be extended to the parties to the present Treaty.

ARTICLE 27. The present Treaty shall be deposited in the archives of the Government of the United States of America which shall furnish each signatory State with a certified copy thereof.

— Reading No. 17 —

SECURITY TREATY BETWEEN THE UNITED STATES OF AMERICA AND JAPAN, 1951 [21]

Since the terms of this treaty were very general, the actual details of the arrangement were left to be worked out later in administrative agreements between the two governments. These arrangements are, therefore, subject to change from time to time.

Security Treaty Between the United States of America and Japan

Japan has this day signed a treaty of peace with the Allied powers. On the coming into force of that treaty, Japan will not have the effective means to exercise its inherent right of self-defense because it has been disarmed.

There is danger to Japan in this situation because irresponsible militarism has not yet been driven from the world. Therefore, Japan desires a security treaty with

---

[21] Department of State Publication 4607, Treaties and Other International Acts Series 2491 (Washington, 1952), pp. 5-6.

the United States of America to come into force simultaneously with the treaty of peace between the United States of America and Japan.

The treaty of peace recognizes that Japan as a sovereign nation has the right to enter into collective security arrangements, and further, the Charter of the United Nations recognizes that all nations possess an inherent right of individual and collective self-defense.

In exercise of these rights, Japan desires, as a provisional arrangement for its defense, that the United States of America should maintain armed forces of its own in and about Japan so as to deter armed attack upon Japan.

The United States of America, in the interest of peace and security, is presently willing to maintain certain of its armed forces in and about Japan, in the expectation, however, that Japan will itself increasingly assume responsibility for its own defense against direct and indirect aggression, always avoiding any armament which could be an offensive threat or serve other than to promote peace and security in accordance with the purposes and principles of the United Nations Charter.

Accordingly, the two countries have agreed as follows:

ARTICLE 1. Japan grants, and United States of America accepts, the right, upon the coming into force of the treaty of peace and of this treaty, to dispose United States land, air and sea forces in and about Japan. Such forces may be utilized to contribute to the maintenance of international peace and security in the Far East and to the security of Japan against armed attack from without, including assistance given at the express request of the Japanese Government to put down large-scale internal riots and disturbances in Japan, caused through instigation or intervention by an outside power or powers.

ARTICLE 2. During the exercise of the right referred to in Article 8, Japan will not grant without the prior consent of the United States of America, any bases or any rights, powers or authority whatsoever, in or relating to bases or the right of garrison or of maneuver, or transit of ground, air or naval forces to any third power.

ARTICLE 3. The conditions which shall govern the disposition of armed forces of the United States of America in and about Japan shall be determined by administrative agreements between the two Governments.

ARTICLE 4. This treaty shall expire whenever in the opinion of the Governments of the United States of America and Japan there shall have come into force such United Nations arrangements or such alternative individual or collective security dispositions as will satisfactorily provide for the maintenance by the United Nations or otherwise of international peace and security in the Japan area.

ARTICLE 5. This treaty shall be ratified by the United States of America and Japan and will come into force when instruments of ratification thereof have been exchanged by them at Washington.

In witness whereof the undersigned plenipotentiaries have signed this treaty.

Done in duplicate at the city of San Francisco, in the English and Japanese languages, this eighth day of September, 1951.

— Reading No. 18 —

EMPEROR HIROHITO AS A POET, 1946-55 [22]

As a people the Japanese have a finely cultivated esthetic sensitivity. This is reflected in the many arts with which they beautify their daily life—flower arrangement (ikebana), *the tasteful hanging scroll painting* (kakemono) *which graces the living room, the potted miniature trees* (bonsai), *the artfully arranged natural stones* (bonseki),

[22] *The New York Times,* January 23, 1946; January 24, 1947; January 2, 1948; February 1, 1950; January 13, 1954; January 1, 1955; slightly modified.

the lovely ceramics, the exquisite colors of the kimono, the landscaped gardens, the clean and honest lines of their dwellings, and the simple decor of their interiors. The most characteristic feature of Japanese art is an overwhelming love of nature. But this love is usually expressed in a carefully pruned and disciplined form. With it goes a tendency to isolate some feature and dwell upon it to the exclusion of everything else.

The traits of Japanese art are well illustrated by Japanese poetry. The Japanese poem is confined to a rigid pattern: the longer form, the tanka, *has 31 syllables in a 5:7:5:7:7 scheme; the shorter form, the* haiku, *has 17 syllables in a 5:7:5 scheme. The object of the poet is to establish a concentrated sense-impression and then with a quick turn of phrase convert this into an emotional response—a most difficult task to accomplish within the brief compass of these forms. It is also part of the requirements that some reference to natural phenomena be included. As with many of the other Japanese arts, poetry writing is not confined to a small group of talented professionals. Skilled writers of* tanka *and* haiku *are to be found in all walks of life, and many Japanese, when in the grip of strong emotions, will turn to poetry to give expression to their feelings. For example, the composition of a* tanka *was one of the last acts performed by General Anami Korechika, the Army Minister, before he committed* hara kiri *in August, 1945.*

An indication of the popularity of the art may be found in the thousands of poems which are entered in the imperial poetry contest held every year in January. The Emperor, who sets the theme of the contest, himself composes an annual poem which is released to the public at this time. Below are seven of the eleven poems which the Emperor has written since the end of World War II. These poems are eagerly studied by many Japanese in the hope of finding some clue to the Emperor's views on current affairs. For instance, the 1946 poem was interpreted as indirectly informing the Japanese people to maintain their true nature despite the adversities of defeat. The 1955 poem was construed as a gesture of support for the Government's austerity program.

1946   Be like pine trees,
        Which do not change color
        Although they bear the weight
        Of continuously falling snow.

1947   The day dawns hopefully
        Upon the town of Mito;
        The sound of the hammer
        Is heard clearly.

1948   Emulate the strength of the pine trees
        On the seashore,
        Which stand the fierce sea breezes
        Of the four seasons.

1948   Learn from the evergreen pine tree:
        In a lonely garden
        In winter decay
        It changes not its color.

1950   The green grasses of spring
        Budding forth with radiant smiles
        On their faces
        Children are seen picking.

1954   As soft the dawn breaks
        Over the still woods
        Of Nazu plain
        Comes the cry of a bird.

1955   Stout are the hearts
        Of the men who toil
        At their honest calling,
        Enduring heat and cold.

A SHORT BIBLIOGRAPHY

Edward A. Ackerman, *Japan's Natural Resources and Their Relation to Japan's Economic Future* (Chicago, 1953).

G. C. Allen, *A Short Economic History of Modern Japan 1867-1937* (London, 1946).

Hugh Borton, *Japan Since 1931* (New York, 1940).

Hugh Borton, ed., *Japan* (Ithaca, 1950).

Hugh Borton and others, *A Selected List of Books and Articles on Japan in English, French and German* (rev. and enlarged, Cambridge, Mass., 1954).

Delmer M. Brown, *Nationalism in Japan* (Berkeley, 1955).

Robert J. C. Butow, *Japan's Decision to Surrender* (Stanford, 1954).

Hugh Byas, *Government by Assassination* (New York, 1942).

Jerome B. Cohen, *Japan's Economy in War and Reconstruction* (Minneapolis, 1949).

Evelyn S. Colbert, *The Left Wing in Japanese Politics* (New York, 1952).

John Embree, *The Japanese Nation* (New York, 1945).

Robert A. Feary, *The Occupation of Japan—Second Phase: 1948-1950* (New York, 1950).

Herbert Feis, *The Road to Pearl Harbor* (Princeton, 1950).

Joseph C. Grew, *Ten Years in Japan* (New York, 1944).

Douglas G. Haring, ed., *Japan's Prospects* (Cambridge, Mass., 1946).

D. C. Holtom, *Modern Japan and Shinto Nationalism* (rev. ed., Chicago, 1947).

Nobutaka Ike, *The Beginnings of Political Democracy in Japan* (Baltimore, 1950).

F. C. Jones, *Japan's New Order In East Asia: Its Rise and Fall 1937-1945* (London, 1954).

William W. Lockwood, *The Economic Development of Japan: Growth and Structural Change 1868-1938* (Princeton, 1954).

Edward M. Martin, *The Allied Occupation of Japan* (New York, 1948).

Walter W. McLaren, *A Political History of Japan During the Meiji Era 1867-1912* (London, 1916).

James Murdoch, *A History of Japan* (3 vols., London, 1925-1926).

E. Herbert Norman, *Japan's Emergence as a Modern State* (New York, 1940).

Edwin O. Reischauer, *The United States and Japan* (Cambridge, Mass., 1950).

Edwin O. Reischauer, *Japan Past and Present* (rev. ed., New York, 1953).

Robert K. Reischauer, *Japan: Government and Politics* (New York, 1939).

G. B. Sansom, *Japan, a Short Cultural History* (rev. ed., New York, 1943).

G. B. Sansom, *The Western World and Japan* (New York, 1949).

Robert Scalapino, *Democracy and the Party Movement in Prewar Japan* (Berkeley, 1953).

Rodger Swearingen and Paul Langer, *Red Flag in Japan* (Cambridge, Mass., 1952).

Tatsuji Takeuchi, *War and Diplomacy in The Japanese Empire* (Chicago, 1935).

Glenn Thomas Trewartha, *Japan: a Physical, Cultural and Regional Geography* (University of Wisconsin, 1945).

Herschel Webb, *An Introduction to Japan* (New York, 1955).

Chitoshi Yanaga, *Japan Since Perry* (New York, 1949).

A. Morgan Young, *Japan in Recent Times 1912-1926* (New York, 1929).

A. Morgan Young, *Imperial Japan 1926-1938* (New York, 1938).

INDEX

Abe, General Nobuyuki, 73
Aikoku Koto, 29
Aikokusha, 29, 30
Ainu, 8, 9
Agrarian disturbances, 15, 26-27, 31
Amaterasu Omikami, *see* Sun Goddess
Amau Statement, 71, 133-36
Anti-Comintern Pact, 75
Army, 23, 27, 38-39, 40, 43, 44, 47-8, 55, 57, 61, 66, 67, 68, 69-70, 72, 73, 74, 79, 83, 86. 107-112; Kwantung —, 67, 71, 72; North China —, 71, 72; *see* Konoe Memorial, Konoe *Memoirs*
Ashida, Hitoshi, 89
Ashikaga Shogunate, 10-11
Australia, 55, 56, 80

Banking, 34, 39, 48, 62, 63
Bonins, 31, 175
Buddhism, 24-25

Cabinet system, 35, 36, 40, 73, 85
Cairo Declaration, 83
Chang, Hsueh-liang, 64, 66
Chang, Tso-lin, 64
Changkufeng, 76
Charter Oath, 22, 99-100
Chemulpo, Treaty of, 41
China, 9, 4, 14, 28, 31; Sino-Japanese War (1894-5), 33, 41-43; Boxer Rebellion, 45; 1911 Revolution, 52; Twenty-one Demands, 53-54, 61, 123-7; 55, 56, 57, 61, 64, 66-7, 70; Sino-Japanese War (1937-1945), 71-2, 77, 78, 79, 80, 81, 82, 88; Communist China, 94; *see* Amau Statement, Inner Mongolia, Konoe *Memoirs,* Manchuria, Shantung, Tanaka Memorial

Choshu, 21, 22, 23
Christianity, 14, 16, 25, 97
Communist Party, Japanese, 63, 89-90
Confucianism, 16, 33
Constitution, Meiji, 30-31, 35, 36-39, 43, 85, 106-107, 114-123
Constitution, 1947, 84-86, 157-172
Court nobles, 9, 20, 22, 27

Daimyo, 10-11, 12, 13, 15, 18, 20, 21, 22, 23, 26, 29, 33, 35; *fudai* —, 11; *tozama* —, 11, 12, 22
Democratic Party, 89, 92
Diet, 36-38, 39, 40, 85
Dodge, Joseph M., 88, 91
Dutch, 14, 17, 18, 77, 78
Dutch Studies, 16-17

Economy, Tokugawa, 15; Early Meiji, 33-35; 1894-1913, 48-50; World War I, 51-52, 54; 1920's, 62-63, 64, 65; 1930's, 74-75; World War II, 80-81; Occupation, 87-89; Post-Occupation, 91-92
Edo, 12, 13, 20, 23
Education, 23-24, 25, 27, 69, 73, 86
Education, Imperial Rescript on, 33, 113-114
Election Law, 37, 44, 61, 84
Emperor, 8, 9, 11, 12, 13, 20, 21, 24, 25, 26, 29, 35, 36, 38, 48, 69, 85, 86-87; *see* Meiji, Hirohito
England, 19, 20, 23, 33, 46, 51, 55, 56, 78, 80, 81, 82; Anglo-Japanese Alliance, 45, 46, 50-1, 56
Eto, Shimpei, 22, 27, 28

Far Eastern Commission, 82
Farm, size of, 13, 49
February 1936 Incident, 69-70

189